COINCIDENCE OR GOD-INCIDENCE?

COINCIDENCE OR GOD-INCIDENCE?

YOU DECIDE

Total Fusion Press,
Strasburg, Ohio

Total Fusion Press
6475 Cherry Run Rd., Strasburg, OH 44680
www.totalfusionpress.com

Printed in the United States of America
24 23 22 21 20 19 18 17 16 15   1 2 3 4 5

ISBN-10: 1-943496-05-6
ISBN-13: 978-1-943496-05-1
Library of Congress Control Number: 2016941679

Editor: Kara Starcher
Front Cover: Pro_Ebookcovers
Interior Design: Kara Starcher

Published in Association with Total Fusion Ministries, Strasburg, OH.
www.totalfusionministries.org

We dedicate this book to our husbands and families for their abundant support and endless patience throughout the arduous process of writing this book.

This book is a living example of a God-incidence. It would not—could not—have happened without God working everyday "coincidences" to bring two of His daughters together to complete this assignment. We dedicate this book to our Heavenly Father, as a testament to His great love for us and the new mercies He has for us each and every day.

Table of Contents

Transformed

Blessed

Acknowledgments

Special thanks to our contributing authors for making this book possible and allowing themselves to be vulnerable by courageously sharing their stories.

What's in It for Me?

How would you answer the question "Does God exist?"

If you answered our question with a "yes," we will call you a believer. You believe and know that only one divine power exists. Maybe your belief in God started recently or maybe you have been a believer for years. Either way, let this book be an encouragement to you in your faith journey as you see evidence of how God works in the lives of everyday people.

If, in your mind, the jury is still out as far as an answer to our question, you are someone that we will call a seeker. You are searching, or seeking, for the answer. The easiest thing for you to do is believe that there is no God, especially if you have never been introduced to Christianity or the teachings of the Bible. Perhaps you are at the other end of the spectrum and once believed in God but someone or something in your life convinced you that God is not real. Do you sometimes wonder if maybe, in the past, you were right and God really does exist? Let this book be a piece of evidence in your pursuit to find the answer to the question—"Does God exist?"

Our contributing authors are everyday people like you. Some of them have been believers all of their lives and can confidently and positively answer the question "Does God exist?" On the other hand, some of our contributors used to be seekers who recently came to believe that God exists. In many cases, their belief came as a direct result of the events they share in their stories. All of our contributors have exhibited vulnerability by sharing their true stories. They have all risked opening themselves up in the hopes that their words may have a transformative power on *your* life.

Whether you consider yourself a believer or a seeker, we invite you to read this collection of stories and decide for yourself if what you're reading is *Coincidence or God-Incidence*. Romans 8:28 says, "And we know that in all things God works for the good of those who love him, who have been called according to his purpose." This book has been our purpose, and we pray that you will find God's imprint in these stories.

How to Use this Book

Coincidence or God-Incidence is divided into four sections—Rescued, Revealed, Transformed, and Blessed. Each section is a collection of personal stories from our contributing authors and illustrates the various ways God shows Himself to us.

At the end of each section are a number of questions intended for personal and/or group reflection. These questions are designed to help you dig a little deeper than the surface of the stories and really think about whether God played a part in the events or if the events merely happened by chance. If you choose to read this book with a group of friends, make sure you set aside some time to discuss the *Reflection Questions* together. If you are reading by yourself, try journaling your answers and, as you do so, ask God to give you a deeper understanding of His power.

We have also included a "challenge" after each section. Once you complete a challenge, interact with us and other readers on our Facebook page (www.facebook.com/GodIncidence) and Twitter (@God_Incidence), telling us your perspective and how the challenge affected you. By sharing your insights, you just might have the opportunity to impact someone through your story and have a positive ripple effect on people you may otherwise never meet.

We truly believe that one or more of the stories in this book will meet you where you're at and will speak to you in a way you may not have anticipated.

If you desire to learn more about God or the Bible, please consult the *Resources* section in the back of the book.

The Story Behind the Stories

Lisa

Have you ever felt like God has been calling you to do something for Him, but you continually make up a mountain of "valid" excuses?

"I'm too busy."
"I'm unqualified."
"I just don't have the financial resources."
"I might fail."

Maybe you've convinced yourself that it wasn't really God—"It's just my own crazy inner voice."

Well, that was me for over ten years. My journey to write *Coincidence or God-Incidence* started years ago when God placed a desire in my heart to write a book capturing His "God stories."

My daughter, who is now twenty-five, was in fifth grade when we walked over to the table at church to sign her up for youth group. In our church, the youth group used a curriculum based out of a book. I quickly found out that the last thing she wanted to do after being in school all day was to sit through another class in the evening. To my surprise, as we approached the sign-up table that Sunday, my normally easy-going, agreeable daughter begged me NOT to sign her up for youth group.

We stepped away from the table so I could listen to her. While I hate to admit it, I took the easy way out. I agreed to let her skip the fifth grade year since we were so busy with Girl Scouts, gymnastics, and dance. To be completely honest, my "taxi cab driver" mom body was just exhausted. But, I made it clear to her that she would be enrolled in youth group the next year.

Fast-forward to sixth grade youth group registration. My daughter and I were walking towards the table and she again pleaded in a whiny voice, "Mom, please don't make me go. It's so boring." I simply reminded her of our agreement from the year before.

As I stood there in the registration line, I heard a whisper in my spirit that very clearly said, "If you're not part of the solution, you're part of the problem."

"What was that?" I thought to myself. "Did I really just hear what I thought I heard?"

My face must have looked puzzled as I began looking around to see who was whispering to me because I doubted that it came from God. However, I knew deep down it wasn't a human whisper, but a whisper that only I could hear. I felt as if God was asking *me* to teach youth group.

In my heart, I answered back, "...but God I'm already so busy." I was the homeroom mom, Girl Scout leader, baseball team mom, fifth grade talent show choreographer—just to mention a few things. To say I was already overcommitted would have been an understatement.

"How am I going to fit this in, God?" I kept arguing in my mind with Him.

Eventually, I finally surrendered to the crazy possibility that this "feeling" might be from the Holy Spirit and not from my own subconscious. At that point, my next step seemed pretty obvious: I started praying about teaching the youth group. I prayed to God and asked Him to give me a sign that He truly wanted me to do this, all the while telling Him that He called the wrong Crumbley, which is my last name. My husband is the teacher, not me. I'm a nurse, and I was terrified at the thought of being in a classroom with thirty 6th graders! But, God knew what He was doing.

At that time, I had a very dear friend with whom I talked every day. Our daughters were the same age and were also friends.

One day while we were chatting, I casually said, "Lori, please don't laugh or think that I'm crazy, but I've been praying about teaching our girls' youth group this year."

She stopped, looked directly at me, and in a slow, almost stunned, voice said, "So have I."

DING DING DING. I knew immediately that God probably laughed at me when I asked Him—the Creator of the universe—for a "sign." However, He gave me exactly what I needed in Lori's answer. It wasn't a coincidence that Lori and I had both been praying about teaching youth group for a while and then revealed it to each other in God's perfect timing.

Lori and I went on to teach three wonderful years of youth group. At the end of those years, I was asked to speak in our church about volunteering. As I was preparing my speech and reflecting back over the previous three years, I heard another whisper in my spirit. It was the call to write this book about stories of ordinary events that God ultimately uses to produce extraordinary outcomes.

During my time of reflection, I realized that so many mountains had to be moved in my life in order for me to be available to teach youth group. For instance, I thought I wasn't going to be able to teach that third year because my daughter had moved up a level in her competitive gymnastics class and the new level met the same night as youth group. I was so discouraged because while I had come to love teaching the youth group kids, I knew I couldn't be in two places at the same time. But God had another plan. Up until that point, the night on which my daughter's new level of gymnastics had always been held was Wednesday evenings. But, it "just so happened" that her class suddenly changed to a different night. *That,* my friends, was not a coincidence.

We all have these "God stories" to tell, but do we ever share them? Do we talk about the ordinary things that God does for us in our lives? Our stories can lift someone's spirit and provide hope and inspiration. Some stories may even, dare I say, help an unbeliever question his or her unbelief and pursue a relationship with Jesus Christ.

When I first felt the desire to write this book all those years ago, I dismissed the "whisper" and told God that He had the wrong girl. As if He didn't know me, I kept trying to convince Him that I wasn't a writer. I was a nurse. I like the sciences; give me anatomy, blood, and guts any day over English and literature. I let the voice of fear inside of me fill me with "valid excuses" for over ten years. *I'm too busy. I wouldn't know where to start. How do I get people to tell me their sto-*

ries? *Aren't there other books out there just like this?* This voice let me believe a lie for years—the lie that I was unqualified to write a book.

Then, in February 2012, I started attending Grace Family Church. One of the first things I did as a member was volunteer in the middle school ministry where I met Brian Levering. Brian's son played in the band and displayed a bold love for God. One day about nine months later, I asked Brian how he planted that kind of love for God in his son's life. Brian simply said, "He saw a miracle happen in me."

As Brian began to tell me his story, I felt a sudden awakening to the assignment God had placed on my heart years before about writing a book. God revealed to me the book's first purpose—**He wanted His stories to be shared.** You see, it was great that Brian told me his story, but I was only one set of ears. I felt in my spirit that many more people needed to hear Brian's story. (You can read Brian's story *4:59* in the *Transformed* section.)

When I heard Brian's story in November 2012, I started praying and seeking encouragement because I still had my doubts and fears about the new uncharted territory of writing books. In January 2013, my pastor, Craig Altman, said something that hit me to the core and confirmed that I needed to be writing. His message was simply "God calls the unqualified." (Isn't it priceless how God always knows what you need when you need it and how sometimes you feel as if a message that is being delivered to a thousand people was meant just for you?)

Pastor Craig's message kicked my motivation into high gear, but before long I started having detours along the way. I quickly became discouraged and thought to myself, "What was I thinking trying to write a book?" The enemy began planting seeds of doubt in my mind. I was trying to open doors to promote the book idea and collect people's stories, but I felt like the doors were not only being shut, but were actually slamming in my face. As a result, I stopped writing and, once again, put my project on the back burner until I heard Pastor Dale Brooks speak on October 20, 2013.

Pastor Dale told about a time when he was visiting his mom in the hospital after she had suffered a stroke. His dad, who was also a pastor, spent time in the hospital chapel praying for his wife. When Pastor Dale joined his dad in the chapel, he listened as his dad recounted all the miracles he had witnessed during his life of ministry. His dad then asked God to perform a miraculous recovery for his wife.

During his sermon, Pastor Dale said, "I wish I'd had a tape recorder to recall all the stories my dad told that day."

As I heard those words, it hit me like a brick. God was revealing to me the book's second purpose—**to preserve our "God stories" so that they aren't lost or forgotten.** After I discovered the book's second purpose, I felt inspired again.

A few months later in February 2014, I was working the Financial Peace University table after one of our church services when I ran into my friend Madelyn Littles. As we chatted, Madelyn told me that she was recently able to quit her job and then told me that she was writing a book. At that moment, I told her I was trying to do the same and asked if we could meet for lunch.

We met within the week, and our lunch lasted about two hours. As I was telling Madelyn my book idea, she became very excited and offered to help. I'd never had this reaction from anyone I had shared my book idea with! Most people wished me well and thought that it was a great idea, but if you know Madelyn, her reaction was over-the-top. Her face lit up and her hands started waving about as she voiced her intense excitement for my book idea.

"Do you want to help me co-author it?" I intuitively blurted out.

"YES!" Madelyn immediately answered, without hesitation.

I've since come to realize that our friendship through Grace Family Church was no accident. Madelyn was destined to be an integral part of this project. Now, more than ten years after I heard that first whisper about writing a book, I know *Coincidence or God-Incidence* wouldn't exist without the people that God placed in my path to help along the way. God's timing was, and always is, perfect.

———— ᖇ .. ᖇ ————

Madelyn

When I ran into Lisa that Sunday, God was already hard at work in my life. I had recently left a job that had become more toxic than I could bear, and I was trying to figure out what my next steps would be. My husband and I had decided that I would take a few months off before starting to look for a new job. In my time off, I had started working on a book that had been on my heart to write for some time. That Sunday after church, when Lisa and I made plans to go to lunch and chat about our projects, I had no idea how the trajectory of my life would change.

During our lunch we discussed our separate book projects, and as Lisa told me more about her book, I felt a pull on my heart. I just knew that this project had to become my sole focus. When Lisa asked me if I wanted to be a part of her project, she asked if I needed to pray about my answer. I immediately told her no. I absolutely didn't need to pray about it because I knew without a doubt that God already had shown me that this was where I was supposed to be spending my time and talents. The book that I was working on was immediately moved to the back burner, and I've not looked back since.

Our first official book meeting happened on February 14, 2014, one week after our lunch meeting. Lisa and I were still getting to know each other, but this project drew us together immediately. We could feel a sisterly bond developing between the two of us.

After our first meeting, things started happening rapidly! For almost a year before we started working together, Lisa had been trying to get some airtime on a local AM radio station. Within weeks of our first meeting, we were asked to be on a daily talk show to share our book idea. It was an amazing experience, but it wasn't just for pleasure— God was working in the background as well. Someone called in to the radio station to share his story with us while we were live on the air! (You can read that story, *Full Circle,* in the *Transformed* section.)

Many years prior, Lisa had been the host of a family health show on Spirit FM, another local station. She tried reaching out to her old colleagues to get some airtime to help collect stories for her book idea. However, she kept running into walls. She sent e-mail after e-mail without getting a response. I encouraged her to send one last e-mail, and within a week, we were scheduled for an on-air interview about the book. (We later found out that Spirit FM experienced issues when they switched e-mail servers, and the intended recipients never even received Lisa's e-mails.)

We prayed that God would make sure that the people who needed to hear the Spirit FM interview would be listening and would be compelled to share their stories. We clearly saw that when God answers a prayer, He answers a prayer! We received an incredible story from a woman who didn't know why she felt nudged to turn on Spirit FM that day, but tuned in anyway. She knew, as she listened to that program, that God wanted her to share her own "God story." (You can read Tammy's story, *A Favor Repaid,* in the *Rescued* section.)

Remember those walls that Lisa kept running into? Well, that was just God setting the stage for His perfect timing. God truly does work in the most amazing, crazy, and mysterious ways.

Lisa

God also has a great sense of humor. He knew all along that I wasn't a writer, but that wasn't an issue for Him. As I mentioned earlier, I'm a nurse and I love the sciences, but God paired me with a librarian who loves English and literature. God sending Madelyn to me just proved, even more so, that I needed to trust in Him. All those years when I was questioning and complaining to Him that I wasn't a writer, He knew that He was going to send me someone who was a perfect match for this project. Even though I couldn't see the future, God had everything planned the whole time.

"'My thoughts are nothing like your thoughts,' says the LORD 'And my ways are far beyond anything you could imagine. For just as the heavens are higher than the earth, so my ways are higher than your ways and my thoughts higher than your thoughts.'" Isaiah 55:8–9 (NLT)

Lisa & Madelyn

Ultimately, we've hoped and prayed three things for this book:

1. Share the stories.
2. Preserve the stories.
3. Watch as God changes the hearts of those who read the stories.

This book in and of itself is a complete testament to God's work in our lives. It is its own example of a God-incidence. God has worked countless little miracles to bring us together at just the right moment to make this book a reality.

RESCUED

Introduction to Rescued

When you see the word *rescued*, what is your first thought?

Did you think of a lifeguard throwing someone a life preserver, an EMT pulling someone from a mangled car, or even something as simple as a friend showing up at the right time to rescue you from an awkward situation? Whatever image came to mind for you, one common denominator exists—a rescue involves *two* people. Have you ever heard of someone running into a burning building to save himself? Of course not! A person runs into a building to save someone else.

How often do we try doing everything on our own and rescuing ourselves? We read self-help books, go on restrictive diets, or proclaim that this is the year we will finally change a bad habit. But we often forget to ask God for His help or guidance. We mistake our pride for strength. We proclaim to the world that we don't need anyone else—including God. However, allowing someone to help, especially in a time of need, isn't a sign of weakness. As Ecclesiastes 4:9–12 says, "Two people are better off than one, for they can help each other succeed. If one person falls, the other can reach out and help. But someone who falls alone is in real trouble. Likewise, two people lying close together can keep each other warm. But how can one be warm alone? A person standing alone can be attacked and defeated, but two can stand back-to-back and conquer. Three are even better, for a triple-braided cord is not easily broken." (NLT)

When we spoke of a rescue involving two people, did it occur to you that maybe God could be *your* Rescuer? He can give you a song at just the right time or show up in the pages of a book. He can send people, sometimes strangers, to help you when you don't even realize you need help. God's rescues can be inconspicuous, showing up in the form of friendship, or they can be easily recognizable, pulling you up from the depths of darkness just when you think you've done something so disgraceful that you are beyond rescuing.

Have you ever felt that you are unforgivable? Maybe you've heard a tiny voice inside your head saying you are unworthy. **You are not alone.** In the following section, you will read stories about rescues from emotional pain and loneliness as well as rescues from physical harm. These stories depict how our contributing authors recognized the help that was placed in their paths and how they chose to accept it. These people realized that they were unable to rescue themselves.

When it comes to being rescued, it takes two.

The Russian Protector

Pixie Hester

The day had finally arrived! For more than a year, over seventy members of our church, Bell Shoals Baptist, had been preparing to go on a mission trip to Russia. Today was the day we were leaving! While there, we planned to join four other churches to visit orphanages, lead worship, teach music, and do prayer walks in various cities.

As I stood in the security line with my group at the Tampa International Airport, I tried practicing my Russian. I'm not very good at speaking the language, and a man in line behind me began laughing at my attempts.

I turned to him with a smile and jokingly asked, "Can you speak better Russian?"

Much to my amazement, he responded in fluent Russian and then said in English, "I'm Boris. Why are you learning Russian?"

I told him about our mission trip, and he shared that he was from Moscow and was visiting Florida on business. As we chatted, I found out that he was friends with the mayor of Ivanovo, the town we would be visiting. He also knew many officials in Moscow, where we would be giving a concert at the end of our trip. What a small world! We continued to chat as we made our way through the security line, but then said goodbye as we went our separate ways to board different flights.

"Piiiixie! Piiiixie!" A few minutes later, while sitting at my gate, I heard someone calling my name. I looked around to see Boris coming my way. "Pixie, here is my card. If you have any problems while you are in my country, give me a call."

I took his card, thanked him, and watched as he walked away.

After a few flight delays, our team finally made it to Moscow. We gathered all of our luggage, went through customs, and exited the airport to find the bus that would drive us five hours to Ivanovo. Much to our surprise, the buses in Russia have very little storage space underneath, and half of our luggage and supplies wouldn't fit. The bus driver wasn't helpful, and we didn't know what to do.

Our worship leader, Simeon, was standing next to a pile of boxes and suitcases taller than he was, trying to figure out a solution.

"Simeon, do you think we should call Boris? He said if we had any problems to call. And, well, this seems to be a problem."

"We don't have any other options," Simeon reluctantly said. "Go ahead and call."

I don't know what Boris did or with whom he may have spoken, but within an hour we had a truck to transport our things.

Once we arrived in Ivanovo, we separated into our various areas of ministry. I was assigned to do prayer walks with a few members of my team while the rest went to a local orphanage to share Bible stories and do activities with the children.

The director of the orphanage asked some of our people to undertake various repair and painting projects. The team wasn't sure if they should do the work because we had religious visas, not work visas, but the director assured them it would be okay.

It turned out that it was *not* okay. The police showed up, separated the men and women into different rooms, took all of their passports, and explained that they were breaking the law.

When my prayer team returned to the orphanage, Simeon tried speaking with the police.

"My team is here doing humanitarian work. We were just trying to brighten up the orphanage for the children." But nothing he said made a difference.

Certain that the rest of our team was going to be thrown into a Russian prison, we were terrified. Once again, I approached Simeon about calling Boris.

Shortly after we spoke to Boris, one of the police officers who was on the scene received a phone call. After he hung up, the officers proceeded to return all of our team's passports—and then told the team they could finish their work!

To this day, I still don't know who Boris contacted or what he told them, but I was grateful that he had once again come to our rescue. I firmly believe that God brought Boris into our lives to protect us because we couldn't have completed the mission trip without Boris' help. It wasn't by chance that Boris heard my feeble attempts at speaking Russian while standing in the airport security line. God had preordained my meeting with our Russian protector.

He also protected us all along the way we went and among all the peoples whose lands we traveled through. Joshua 24:17b (HCSB)

—————— ∿ ·· ∾ ——————

The Light
in the Darkness

Shonie Welker

—————— ∿ ·· ∾ ——————

I was a military brat who didn't have faith in God. I embodied the objectivist mindset, meaning I believed everyone's actions were done to gain personal happiness.

While growing up, my family moved around a lot. From a young age, I developed a jaded view of the world because, in my experience, people were expendable. Relationships weren't necessary and only brought pain. As a result, I threw myself into my studies, hoping for a better future—one that would overshadow the loneliness and pain I felt. I always told myself that when I settled down I would make friends and the pain would go away, but that wasn't the case. When I went off to college, I continued to lose myself in my studies, but I struggled against the loneliness. I imagined that once I graduated from college every door would begin to open and the hurt would suddenly disappear. But, that wasn't the case.

I made one friend, but having a friend didn't seem to fight off the darkness that overwhelmed me. Some days I stared at the ceiling and hours passed by. I couldn't pinpoint why I was so sad or why I had a sense of worthlessness. I felt like a walking zombie with the weight of the world sitting upon my shoulders. Negativity consumed my thoughts. Each and every day was a struggle.

At one point thoughts of suicide overtook my mind. I came up with what I thought was the perfect plan. I knew exactly how I would end my life. I just didn't know when I would do it. The only thing that kept me from leaving this earth was my family. I felt joy when I was with them, and the thought of how much I would hurt my family prevented me from killing myself. I didn't want to cause them pain.

My mother frequently suggested that I visit the local church, but I was against going. Eventually, however, I gave in and ended up at church on a Wednesday night because I wasn't sure how much longer I could fight the darkness within myself. My only reason for going that night was to make my mom feel better should I decide to commit suicide.

As I sat in my car in the church parking lot, fear consumed me and negative thoughts swarmed in my head.

"What if they don't like me?"

"What if they turn me away?"

"What if they realize I know nothing about the Bible?"

I opened my car door, shut it, and opened it again. Finally, I called my mom, and in typical mom fashion, she encouraged me to get out of my car. I took a deep breath and put my feet on the ground.

Just then a car pulled into the parking space next to me. A woman exited the vehicle, took one look at me, smiled, and asked if it was my first time coming to the church. I reluctantly admitted that it was. I waited for her to pass judgment, but she didn't. Instead she walked me straight inside the doors of the church and all the way down to the front of the auditorium. Sitting close to the front was a little too much for me, so I moved to a seat in the back.

While I was sitting by myself in the back of the auditorium, the familiar darkness found me again. Feeling all alone, I decided to leave and head home. At that point in the service, the pastor told everyone to greet their neighbors. The lady who had walked in with me came up to me before I could leave, grabbed me by the hand, and practically dragged me to the front of the church. The darkness seemed to abate a little. Then the pastor asked the congregation to split up in small groups. I met some wonderful people in my group, which to me was amazing because I didn't think any good people were left in the world. When the service concluded, I decided I would attend the next Sunday service.

On Sunday morning, I cautiously walked into the church and took a seat. The pastor began to speak, and during his sermon he talked about how, at one point, he had attempted suicide and how he eventually found God. As the pastor shared his experience, tears fell down my face. At the end of the service, the pastor invited everyone to come to the front of the church to pray with the prayer team. Somehow my feet found their way to the front where I stood looking at a prayer team member. I think I asked her to pray for strength for me, but I really didn't even know what I was asking for. I know that God gave her the words to pray over me because they were exactly what I needed. We held each other's arms, and as the prayer escaped from her mouth, I felt the darkness, the heaviness, being lifted from my shoulders. I felt ten times taller. I felt happy! I felt even happier than I did when I was with my family. Joy emanated from within.

It was no coincidence that the woman who pulled up next to me in the parking lot knew that I needed additional encouragement to enter the church. It was no coincidence that the pastor spoke about suicide that Sunday. It was no coincidence that the prayer team member knew exactly what to pray over me. God knew what I needed, and He made a way for it to happen.

Since that day, I've never had to battle that all-consuming darkness again. Yes, I get sad at times, but never so sad that I don't see a reason to live. I found God, the light that brought me out of the darkness. I don't struggle with negative thoughts anymore—I'm truly happy. It is a happiness that can only come from Him.

For he has rescued us from the kingdom of darkness and transferred us into the Kingdom of his dear Son. Colossians 1:13 (NLT)

Saturdays with Helen

Donna Kattner

Each year on Easter Sunday I place flowers on my parents' and grandparents' graves. They are buried in separate cemeteries that are equal distances from my house but in opposite directions. One particular year, I didn't have a specific plan, so I wasn't sure which cemetery to visit first. For no discernible reason, I decided to start at the cemetery where my maternal grandparents are buried.

I was standing by their gravesite when I looked up to see a familiar figure walking towards me. Helen, a well-loved member of the church where I previously attended, was in her 80s and had lived all her life across the street from the church and the cemetery. I always knew her as the pretty lady who loved dogs and always had a smile for everyone, especially babies. In her younger days, her beauty would have given Marilyn Monroe a run for her money.

Helen had been involved with many church and family groups over the years, and I grew to know her through a group called "The Crafters." Our group made things to sell at the church's annual bazaar. It wasn't so much the making of crafts that made this group so wonderful, but rather the friendship and laughter—and Helen's presence.

That day at the graveside, Helen and I started chatting, and one of the first questions Helen asked was "How is Bill?" (Bill was my significant other.) I burst into tears. Helen knew that Bill had dealt with some major health issues, and she immediately asked if something had happened to him. I assured her that Bill was okay, but I was devastated about our recent breakup. Helen invited me back to her house to talk some more. I sobbed and cried and laughed with Helen that day, and I used up a bunch of her tissues.

Later that afternoon as I was leaving her home, Helen asked me to come to the next Saturday evening church service with her. Since Helen's church had a smaller congregation and she hadn't seen me there in awhile, she knew that I had stopped coming. I agreed to attend the service with her, and a new Saturday night tradition began. Helen and I went to church together and then back to her house for some snacks, some tears, and lots of laughter. She became my Saturday night fix.

Sadly, Helen has since passed on, but I still carry on the tradition of going to Saturday night service.

Looking back, I believe God directed my steps that day to visit the cemetery across from Helen's house first so that Helen would cross my path. Isn't it wonderful how God knows just what—or who—we need, when we need it? He placed Helen in my life so that I could heal and become the person He wanted me to be.

In their hearts humans plan their course,
but the LORD establishes their steps. Proverbs 16:9

A Favor Repaid

Tammy Wilkins

At the age of twenty-two, I was a stay-at-home mom for my two young children, ages three and four. One day, my husband abandoned our family, leaving us with no source of income and hardly any money. As a result, we were evicted from our rented home.

I found a job in Tampa, Florida, an hour away from where we currently lived, but the low wages and the small amount of welfare I received were simply not enough to keep us afloat. I found myself in a desperate situation. I had no child support, no home, and nowhere to go. I drove around my small town for a few hours one night, trying to decide what to do. I had no idea where my children and I were going to sleep that night.

Finally I drove to a pay phone and began calling apartment complexes located in Tampa. It didn't take long for me to realize that all the apartments were much more expensive than the $350 I could afford. On the verge of giving up, I dialed one last phone number.

A woman answered, and she explained that I would need to pay the first and last months' rent along with a deposit. Once again I felt desperation rise up within me. It was simply too much money. I thanked her and explained that I couldn't afford that amount because my monthly check from the state was simply not enough.

I was about to hang up when she said, "Wait, did you say you had two babies?"

"Yes," I replied. "I do."

What she said next shocked me!

"If you bring me the check," she said, "I will allow you to move in today, and I will cover the rest."

I hung up and called back because I was stunned that a total stranger would be willing to help when my own husband had abandoned us.

With my children in tow, I rushed to the apartment complex an hour away. The lady allowed us to move in along with all of our possessions, which amounted to a garbage bag of clothes, one twin bed, a frying pan, a bowl, two plates, and two plastic glasses.

Over the next five years, I put my life back together. I re-dedicated my life wholly to God, who blessed me in many ways and provided me a job working in a childcare center. I began attending and serving in a local church. Even though I was happily living my new life, I still never forgot the woman who had helped me, and I prayed for the opportunity to someday repay her for her kindness.

One afternoon during a work staff meeting, a teacher mentioned that twin girls in her class were being raised by their grandparents. The grandmother had inquired if any of the teachers at the center would be willing to take care of the girls for a weekend to provide the grandparents with some much needed rest. I quickly volunteered and was told that I would soon be able to meet the grandmother.

About a week later, I was called from my classroom to meet the grandmother of the girls. After introductions, we made small talk, and I asked her where she worked and what she did.

"I'm an apartment manager here in town," she said. Then she gasped. "You're the girl that I helped all those years ago!"

We hadn't immediately recognized one another as the years had changed us both, but once we realized our connection, we both started to cry. We hugged each other and shared our unbelievable story with the other teachers. Everyone was amazed—they too knew this was much more than coincidence.

My family had a wonderful time with the twins that weekend, and it gave the grandparents the break that they needed. I'm so grateful that God answered my prayer and allowed me the opportunity to repay this woman who had helped me and my family when we needed it most.

The LORD is good, a refuge in times of trouble.
He cares for those who trust in him. Nahum 1:7

This story was originally published in *Overflow* magazine as "No Such Thing As Coincidence" in February 2011. It is adapted and reprinted here with permission of the author and courtesy of *Overflow*.

Healing from My Secret Sin

Brandee Nielsen

In September 2014, I attended an annual three-day women's retreat hosted by my church in Tampa, Florida. I had been a member of the church for three years and usually let this event pass me by. But this year was different. For the first time I felt pulled to attend and I registered without question.

When I arrived at the retreat, I began to wonder what God had in store for me. I realized that He had led me there, but I had no idea why. I decided not to over-analyze the possibilities and just roll with the schedule.

My welcome folder contained the itinerary describing each day's events. One of the events was titled "Late Night Chats," which were breakout sessions tailored to women experiencing specific circumstances. When I looked over the list, I identified with some of the session topics. Two of them addressed issues that were personal to me—ones for which I was well into my journey of healing, and I smiled when I saw them.

"I could go to either one of those!" I said to myself.

Then I looked at the next topic. "Oh no! Not that. No way am I even walking into that room!"

I continued reading through the itinerary, and several daytime sessions caught my attention. I made a decision to attend one titled "You've Got the Power." The session was all about the impact our words have on ourselves and on others. At the end of the session, the leaders, Lisa and Madelyn, shared an opportunity to submit personal stories for potential inclusion in a book they were writing. I had already written and published my own life story, but I still felt compelled to fill out the interest card.

That evening when it was time to decide if I would either call it a night or look at the "Late Night Chat" sessions again, it became clear that God wanted me to go through that self-proclaimed forbidden door. In a flash I understood why I was at the women's retreat. I had a hidden secret in my past that I hadn't surrendered to God or shared with others. A secret that kept me so fearful and ashamed that I didn't even write about it in my own book. It was a sin I had locked away and silently suffered from for twenty-five years. God revealed to me that I was at the women's retreat because He wanted to heal me completely by revealing the truth about my secret. He wanted to free me from the bondage I suffered.

I trusted God's leading and walked into the chat titled "Surrendering the Secret: A Journey to Healing from Abortion." Not only did I attend that chat, but I then enrolled in the group study on the same topic. Over the next several weeks, I learned how much God truly loves me and how much He loved me through my wrong choices twenty-five years ago. In the group studies, I discovered that the price for sin had already been paid—even for my sin of abortion. I learned that it was okay to share my secret about abortion. Like the leaders of the "You've Got the Power" session emphasized, my words had power, and sharing my secret with others helped me find healing. For every person reading this who can identify with the pain and shame of abortion, and even those who can't, I'm compelled, honored, and obligated to share my story with you.

I was nineteen years old the first time I got pregnant. I had been using birth control pills and likely missed taking it one day in the cycle. It was an honest mistake. I was three months along when I received my blood test results confirming the pregnancy. As a believer, I accepted my pregnancy, telling God that if He needed a child to be born, it would be safe with me because I would never have an abortion. When I was five months pregnant, I married my baby's father, but we divorced before our baby's second birthday. I was a single mom by the time I was twenty-two years old.

Then one day, I met a successful, charming guy at the gym. He was twenty-five years old, a graduate of a prestigious university where he had been a football player, and was now a president of a bank branch. He was very romantic and swept me off of my feet. We began dating and fell in love.

One day he asked me if I would move in with him. I agreed, and my child and I moved in. Then, he proposed, and we got engaged. Not long after, he requested that I quit my job as a Pre-K teacher at the same school where my child attended so that I could stay home with my child and be a housewife. I agreed.

After I stopped working outside of the home, my fiance became increasingly controlling in every aspect of my life. He was very jealous that my child wasn't his own and told me he wanted to have a child together. I reluctantly agreed because of his overbearing personality. Each night when he arrived home from work, he demanded sex until I became pregnant. I was very young and fragile, without a job, and completely dependent on him.

When I missed the first day of my period the following month, I purchased a pregnancy test from the drug store. Even with my fiance's demands and his attitude toward my child, I was excited about the prospect of having another baby. I followed the test instructions and stood staring at the little window hoping for a positive result. My heart leaped with joy as I realized I was pregnant. I immediately went back to the drug store and bought a package of infant diapers and some gift wrap. I placed the positive pregnancy test inside a diaper and wrapped it as a surprise for my fiancé.

When he walked into the house that evening, I handed him the gift. He opened the gift and quickly dropped it on the table. His reaction was a mixture of shock, a bit of fear, somewhat happy and somewhat concerned. I thought his reaction would be more positive.

Almost immediately, his controlling behavior and jealousy over my first child having a different father became worse. He demanded that I legally revoke my first child's father's rights so that he could adopt my child. When I refused, he threatened to beat me. He told me that we wouldn't get married, and that he would take his baby away from me once it was born. I panicked. This was beyond any situation I had ever experienced before. I was afraid for my life, my first child's life, and now my unborn baby's life. I knew I was in trouble.

One afternoon, while my fiancé was outside mowing the lawn, I seized the opportunity to escape the horrendous situation. I quickly packed a few necessary items for me and my child and slipped out the door. My fiancé heard the car and tried to run after me, but I was on my way to a safe house before he could stop us.

My despair over my situation turned my thoughts upside down. I decided that my best option was to abort my unborn baby because then he or she would not be hurt by this man and could never be taken away from me. I thought that since abortion was legal and that the baby was, as they say, merely a blob of tissue in the early stages of gestation, it was an accepted and right thing to do in my situation. I believed that abortion was the remedy I needed so that my first child and I could cut all ties with my fiancé. So, I privately sought an abortion provider and made the appointment.

I was nine weeks pregnant. What I didn't know then was that by this time my baby's heart was already beating and all of its essential body parts were developed. I remembered my promise to God when I was pregnant with my first child—if He wanted a child to be born, it would be safe with me. The week before the abortion, darkness began to consume me. Every day I sat in a dark room, starving myself and praying to God to please remove the soul of this child from its body before I killed it by abortion. I was crushed into a million pieces. I loved and wanted my baby, but not under these circumstances.

After I had the abortion, my life was never the same. I punished myself and became anorexic, which eventually led to body image disorder, exercise bulimia, and vanity issues that took on a life of their own. I felt worthless. I felt God would never forgive me for breaking my promise and aborting His gift of life. Nothing mattered anymore.

Three years later I found myself pregnant again. This time the circumstances didn't include an abusive man; the timing was just wrong in the lives of two young people. Misguided again and believing it was the right thing to do, I had another abortion. This time I was seven weeks pregnant. Since I had already had one abortion and felt worthless, I went through it again, resolved to having sealed my fate as an unforgivable soul.

The second abortion only added to my unspeakable pain and darkness, anchoring me in my self-condemnation and perpetual doom. I grieved the loss of my two unborn babies for many years until my body image disorder and insecurity issues consumed me. Then I put the abortions behind me, shoving them way down deep and never addressing them again, all the while believing I would never be forgiven until I attended that "Late Night Chat."

When I look back at that once-brave young girl who turned desperate and aborted two children, I now fully understand that I had better options for those babies. I wish I could go back and save myself from making those two painful mistakes. I wish I could see those children. I want to tell them I'm so sorry for taking their lives just so I wouldn't have to deal with the stress and difficulties of allowing them to live. I know now that I was wrong, and I was selfish. I also cheated myself out of the opportunity to hold them, to watch their little eyes open for the first time to see me smiling back at them, saying, "Hello, I'm your mommy." I dream about who they'd be today and what our lives would have been like while they grew up. The laughter, the love, the hard times would have all been for the good of my life and theirs.

I thank God for leading me to that women's retreat. That "Late Night Chat" and subsequent study showed me how God could rescue me from my pain, guilt, and self-condemnation. I willingly embraced God's love and forgiveness, and today I'm healed and forgiven.

¹ Blessed is the one whose transgressions are forgiven,
whose sins are covered.
² Blessed is the one whose sin the LORD
does not count against them
and in whose spirit is no deceit.
³ When I kept silent, my bones wasted away
through my groaning all day long.
⁴ For day and night your hand was heavy on me;
my strength was sapped as in the heat of summer.
⁵ Then I acknowledged my sin to you
and did not cover up my iniquity.
I said, "I will confess my transgressions to the LORD."
And you forgave the guilt of my sin.
Psalm 32:1–5

Connect With The Contributing Author

Brandee is a muscian, songwriter, author, speaker, and blogger.
Website: www.brandeenielsen.com
E-mail address: brandee@brandeenielsen.com

Rescued Reflection Questions

1. Can you think of a time when God placed someone in your path to help rescue you from physical or emotional pain, illness, or harm? If so, who rescued you? What were you rescued from?

_____

_____

_____

_____

2. Which of the stories in this section can you most closely relate to? Why?

_____

_____

_____

_____

3. In the beginning of this section, we talked about how a rescue takes two people. Are you allowing others to help in your time of need or are you trying to do it all alone?

_____

_____

_____

_____

4. Can you identify any obstacles that are keeping you from accepting help? Some examples of roadblocks are pride, fear, unforgiveness, self-condemnation, and feelings of unworthiness.

_____

_____

_____

_____

5. In *Healing from My Secret Sin,* Brandee was able to break the chains of guilt and shame from her past. What chains from your past are still unbroken?

_____

_____

_____

_____

Challenge

In the section introduction, we used the words **You are not alone.** If you would like to share a time when you realized that you were not alone, when God intervened to rescue you, we invite you to post to our Facebook page (www.facebook.com/GodIncidence) or Twitter account (@God_Incidence) with the hashtag #CoincidenceChallenge.

REVEALED

Introduction to Revealed

If you've ever watched a home makeover show on television, you know that the grand finale of each episode showcases a big reveal. During the course of the show, the homeowners experience the ups and downs that come with a home renovation. They eagerly anticipate their space being completed. When the new look is revealed, the homeowners are amazed, often to the point of tears. No longer forced to look at what was there before, the homeowners see something brand new, something they never could have imagined without a skilled design and construction team.

The meaning of the word *revealed* implies that something was once covered or hidden from view. Before construction begins in the home makeover, the design team shows the homeowners mock-ups of what their new space will look like, but the final result isn't clear until the work is finished and everyone sees the room for the first time—the big reveal. The same is true in the making of a new quilt. When a quilter first begins, the random pieces of fabric lying before her are just that—random. Yet she has a vision and a design for what she wants that quilt to look like. Even as she starts to sew those seemingly random pieces into blocks, with each block having its own pattern, the final design remains obscure and hidden from view. Piece by piece the quilter painstakingly continues until, finally, she sews together the last of the blocks, revealing the quilt's true beauty and intricacy.

God works in the same manner. At times, He gives us glimpses of the blueprints He has for our lives. These glimpses may seem like random pieces of fabric or a home under construction, and, like a puzzle, we may only be able to define the corners and borders at first. Then, slowly, we begin to see the pieces come together, and eventually, at some point in the future, the whole picture is revealed to us.

God often prepares a way for us long before we even realize it. He sets things in motion—days, weeks, and sometimes even years in advance. And He oftentimes chooses to reveal Himself to us when we least expect it. Our local church pastor certainly didn't think he would hear from God at age nineteen while sitting on a barstool and downing yet another beer. But that was God's perfect timing. Pastor Craig listened to the whisper he heard in that smoky bar, and it changed his life. As time has revealed, his obedience also changed the lives of thousands of people who have come to know Christ through the church Pastor Craig and his wife founded.

As we begin to seek and know God, we gradually become more conscious of the many ways in which He reveals Himself to us—perhaps through a dream, as in *The Unusual Dream*, or a perfectly timed message as in *A Shred of Hope*. In the following stories, you will see how God reveals Himself to ordinary people. Is your heart open to the idea of God revealing Himself to you?

——— ᘐ··ᘡ———

A Shred of Hope

Margaret in the Mountains

——— ᘐ··ᘡ———

As a child, I lived in a Christian home. We attended church regularly, and I memorized many Bible verses throughout my childhood. Little did I know that as an adult those scriptures would be my source of strength in the midst of a major life crisis.

At age eighteen, I married my high school sweetheart. My only goal in life at that time was having a successful marriage and raising our children. Thirty years later, my husband and I were still happily married, or so I thought. After all, we had a large, lovely home and two educated and married daughters.

Early one evening in December, a stranger knocked on our front door. When I answered the door, this stranger handed me a stack of papers—for a divorce. I thought surely the papers must be a joke or that the individual had the wrong address. My husband and I had had no prior discussions about divorce! But it wasn't a joke. The papers were real.

To say I was devastated would be a massive understatement. I lived in a daze of confusion for the next few weeks. I struggled to accept the reality of my circumstances because I had been reared to believe that marriage was for life. When I said "I do," I knew, for me, it would be for better or worse, richer or poorer, and until death parted us.

After the initial shock wore off, I felt so guilty. I continually asked myself what I had done wrong and what I could have done differently. I drew upon my early teachings for the strength and courage to face each day. Over time, I learned to let go and let God show me the way through this devastating period of my life.

The healing of my broken heart began in an empty bedroom during a bout of overwhelming sadness. My father-in-law, Papa, had lived with us for about five years, and when my husband left, he moved Papa to a local assisted living facility. I had been very close to Papa and missed him very much. One particular evening, I walked into Papa's empty bedroom, hoping to find comfort. On the bedroom floor lay a small strip of paper—the type that would be cut from a Bible study or Sunday School program.

I thought to myself, "It must have fallen out of Papa's Bible, but how can that be?" I knew I had long since cleaned his room, vacuumed the floor, and packed up his remaining belongings.

I picked up the paper, turned it over, and read, "Sometimes relationships are broken and can't be fixed." The scripture reference was Jeremiah 3.

Later, I sat down to read Jeremiah 3 and had a breakthrough. That Bible chapter helped me to understand that my husband had changed—and there was nothing I could do to change him back. God was telling me to accept my predicament. I no longer needed to feel guilty about a broken marriage I couldn't fix.

Once I knew God's will was for me to accept my situation, I focused on things that needed to be done to move forward with my life. On many occasions I felt God's loving presence with me during my despair, and He gave answers just when I needed them. God was there to help me every step of the way, and I'm truly blessed today. I now believe that there is no such thing as coincidence. God is in control, and everything happens for a reason, even things as small as finding a scrap of paper.

But blessed is the one who trusts in the LORD,
whose confidence is in him. Jeremiah 17:7

An Unusual Dream

Pam Wolf

I was raised unchurched.

Actually, if the truth be told, I guess I was raised "heathen." Unchurched is just a nicer way of saying it.

Don't get me wrong, I came from good, hardworking mid-westerners. We went to church on the obligatory holidays of Easter and Christmas, and since I wasn't born Jewish, I figured I must be a "Christian." I simply had no idea that there was anything more to being a Christian than calling myself one.

But even then, this God who I didn't yet know was already playing a role in my life through two very special women—my aunt and my great-grandmother. They both loved going to church and took me when I visited them, and although they never really spoke of their faith, I know they must have prayed for me and hoped one day I, too, would "catch it."

In fact, years later when I married, my aunt planted God's Word in my hands when she gave me my first Bible. A King James, no less! In gratitude and a bit out of curiosity, I attempted to read it, but I only made it to somewhere around Genesis 3. I laid it down wondering how anyone could ever make it through a book that long and difficult to read!

As life does for all of us, the years marched along. For me, those years came with great success, both financially and professionally. However, my personal life was an entirely different kind of story. In the wake of all the striving, I found myself divorced, raising two children, and leaning on my sweet mother to help fill the gaps. I was determined to do things my way. Going to church wasn't part of my plan.

That's when I met Tom.

His resume was a lot like mine—success in the business world and financially, but not in life or marriage. Unlike me, he was raised in church with enough visits to mass and confession that he had decided he was done with all that.

So, two "do it yourself - I can make it happen" people came together and decided to try to make the relationship part of their lives "work." Having both gone through bad divorces, we were determined to be "really sure" this time and decided it would be best if we try living together first. You know, if you are going to buy the shoe, you have to try it on, right?

Five years later, still trying to make our crazy life work, still trying to blend a "sort of" family, we decided it was time to make a real commitment and get married. One thing we felt by that point was that we didn't want this relationship to fail. We were determined to make this marriage work. Somewhere deep down we wanted to prove to ourselves and show our children that a lasting marriage was actually possible.

Finally married, we each continued to climb the ladders of success.

We built our dream home in a beautiful, upscale, gated community. At the time, Tom's daughter Megan was already in college, my daughter Amanda was in middle school, and my son Nick was a junior in high school. He had one more year before he would go off to Florida State University (FSU).

We had been living in our new home for a year when I began to wonder if some of Nick's behavior and antics, which we had been chalking up to senior-itis and teenage experimentation, were actually something more serious. I was afraid for Nick, but I didn't know what was wrong or how to help him. I would later learn that this was part of his ten-year foray into deep drug and alcohol addiction.

I relied on my own wisdom in my attempts to help Nick. I hoped that college would be the antidote to his problems and would help him get back on track. Yet, without knowing it, I was letting him go out the door to FSU wholly unprepared. He was stepping onto a dangerous, self-destructive path—alone.

Six months later, I was invited to a neighborhood Christmas party where I met Teri. She was sweet, kind, and friendly. She eagerly pulled me aside and began telling me about all the activities in our neighborhood—the women's club, the golf and bridge groups, and oh, by the way, a women's Bible study.

"Hmmm," I thought, "Everyone should probably read the Bible at least once in her lifetime. And this Bible study could be a great place to meet some new friends and neighbors!"

Since I still hadn't cracked open that Bible my aunt gave me all those years ago except for my first attempt at reading it, I figured I would go ahead and try the Bible study. When I told Tom I was thinking of joining the group, he looked at me with great surprise and said, "You've got to be kidding!"

I guess it was pretty surprising, all things considered.

As I continued to think about going, doubts and second thoughts filled my mind. Maybe I shouldn't go after all. And if I did go, "they" would surely see me for who I really was. I would be the woman with the big red "S" all over her...you know, sinner extraordinaire. "They," on the other hand, would be those perfect Christian people who have it all together. And surely they would be judging me.

If it weren't for Teri coming by to pick me up that first day, I probably wouldn't have gone.

Once there, I soon realized how wrong I was about these women. They were incredibly kind, and a lot of them had everyday troubles just like I did. Some were even divorced and remarried, just like me. They were willing to be transparent about their struggles. They prayed for each other. I had never seen people do that!

And then God gave me Grace, the woman leading the study. We were almost instant friends (and remain so today). As she mentored me, the more I learned and the more I wanted to know. But I will admit that it was difficult for me in the beginning—it seemed as if Christians spoke a foreign language with all kinds of words and phrases I didn't understand. So, at Grace's instruction, I kept a notepad, wrote down all my questions, and brought them to her for answers and insight. Here's the cool thing—Grace never gave me her answers. She always began by opening the Bible and then helping me find my answers in the text. Over time, I came to realize that every answer I needed for my life was in that book!

As I continued in the Bible study, I kept sharing everything I was learning with Tom, who was slowly gaining new interest in the things of God. Tom eventually began attending the men's neighborhood Bible study facilitated by Grace's husband.

As I look back, this time in my life was both the best of times and the worst of times. The best of times included our beautiful new home, the wonderful people Tom and I were meeting, and our growing appreciation for God and His Word. But it was still the worst of times as I continued to watch my son struggle. Although I was getting to know the Lord, I felt like I couldn't help my son Nick and that somehow I had missed my opportunity to share true wisdom with him.

One day, as I was sitting in my beautiful new living room, gazing out arched windows into the sunlit sky, I said to myself, "There must be someone up there who has blessed me. All that I have—this must be a gift from God, right?"

Yet, at the same time, I was telling God, "I cannot do this alone. I want a better relationship with my step-daughter. I have another little girl who is growing up, and I don't want to fail her. If there is any way, if it's not too late for my son, I would be so very grateful for Your help and guidance there, too."

The next day, June 13, 2001, I woke up early from an odd but interesting dream. In my dream I was making homemade yeast bread with my grandmother just like we did when I was a child. The odd thing was that the yeast had become so aggressive that the dough just kept multiplying. I was busy handing my fourteen-year-old daughter big sections of the dough, asking her to help as my grandmother and I tried to keep up with the kneading process.

As I dressed that morning, I passed it off as a silly dream. Later that day as I was driving to a friend's house, I heard a pastor on the radio talking about how the Bible often refers to yeast as sin. He said it takes only a little "sin" to infect the whole batch of dough. His words hit me like a ton of bricks.

I immediately thought about my dream and handing the dough to my young daughter—dough that was infected with sin. I pulled my car to the side of the road and began to sob uncontrollably. I knew right then and there that I hadn't just had a silly dream the night before. It was a message from the God about my life. I realized that I had been teaching my children the ways of the world and not the wisdom of God. Then I heard God say, "Pam, there is still time!"

June 13, 2001, wasn't just another day that started with a random dream. It was how God began speaking to me; it was the beginning of subsequent circumstances that would help my dream make more sense. Ultimately, that day led to my salvation. God used my dream to show me how much I needed Him. He let me know that if I would turn my life over to Him, He would fill the empty place in my soul that nothing else had ever been able to fill.

By God's grace, my husband also came to know the Lord a month later. My family tree has drastically changed—forever—because I decided to accept a simple invitation to a neighborhood Bible study. My ninety-one-year-old mom, along with my step-dad, my sister, and my niece have all come to know Jesus. All three of our children have a relationship with our Lord and are married to God-loving spouses. Megan, who is now thirty-six, is being given the grace to raise a child with special needs. Nick, who is now thirty-two, has been sober for seven years, and Amanda, who is twenty-nine, is courageously fighting—and winning—her battle against inflammatory breast cancer. Praise God!

Get rid of the old yeast so that you may be a new batch of dough, since you are to be free from yeast. 1 Corinthians 5:7a (ISV)

Story adapted from *Identity and Destiny: 7 Steps to a Purpose- filled Life.* Originally published 2011. Rebranded and titled 2014—*Finding Your God-given Sweet Spot.* Used by permission of Pam Wolf, Author

Connect With The Contributing Author

Pam is an author, speaker, and business coach.
Websites: www.identityanddestiny.com
www.tomandpamwolfcoaching.com
E-mail: pam@identityanddestiny.com
facebook.com/IdentityandDestiny
twitter.com./godspurpose4u

Hidden Treasure

Marie Halladay

The lovely little house in the country where I grew up had stood vacant for several years, as often happens when parents grow older. My father had died after a long illness, and my mother, who had struggled to maintain the little house for such a long time, finally succumbed to the need to move into a personal care home.

My three siblings and I were faced with the unpleasant task of disposing of the house and its possessions. Together we decided on a public auction. We carefully scrutinized the many items left in the home, wishing to preserve those items that had special memories or sentimental value. We considered anything relating to our ancestors or heritage as especially important, not only to us, but also to pass on to our children.

On the day of the auction, I sat in my mother's yard watching the people, many of them neighbors and friends, bid on my mother's goods. I was very saddened to see items that had been valued so highly by my mother being sold for a pittance. However, some of the items were nothing more than junk, and the auctioneer had difficulty getting even a small bid.

One such item was a plastic laundry basket loaded with odd kitchen utensils, some puzzle boxes, electrical cords, and other items of little value. When the auctioneer was unable to obtain even a twenty-five cent bid, he added my mother's dough board for a package deal.

After quick consideration, I decided it might be nice to own the board on which my mother had lovingly rolled so many delicious pie crusts. I must admit I don't even remember what I bid for the items, but I know it was nominal. However, what I found after buying it wasn't nominal—it was priceless!

I was happy to have my dough board, but eager to dispose of the junk in the laundry basket, so I headed for the nearest garbage can. As I was about to discard the puzzle boxes, a little voice inside me told me to remove the lids. When I did, I stared in astonishment!

Instead of the puzzle pieces I expected to find, I found pictures of our ancestors dating back to the 1800s. These irreplaceable pictures were of relatives I had never met, including my grandparents. One was of my grandfather driving a horse-drawn milk wagon, and another of my grandmother who died at the age of twenty-eight during the flu epidemic of 1917. I discovered pictures of my mother and her brothers and sisters as infants and toddlers as well as graduation pictures, wedding pictures, and so much more.

Later, I asked myself, "Was it luck that no one bid on the laundry basket? What moved the auctioneer to add the dough board to the goods? Why was I even paying attention to the bidding at that particular moment?"

Was it a fluke—a stroke of luck? I don't think so. I'm still amazed when I think about it. I truly believe our Lord was there in the midst of the hustle and bustle of that auction. I believe He wanted me to have those pictures and miraculously wove together a set of events to achieve that end.

*I will give you hidden treasures, riches stored in secret places,
so that you may know that I am the LORD, the God of Israel,
who summons you by name.* Isaiah 45:3

Bringing Garret Home

Jennifer Greer

After my first marriage ended, I never thought I would feel safe enough to love another man again, but God, who was my best friend, had other plans. Seven years later I met a man who would eventually become my husband. Ben showed me a glimpse of what I believe God's unconditional love looks like. When Ben and I married, God blessed me with two new daughters who were the same ages as my two children. It's like we had two sets of twins.

On Saturday, June 7, 2014, while our family was vacationing at the beach, God brought someone else into our lives. Ben and I were sitting on the beach with the sun shining and a cool breeze blowing. I was listening to my favorite sound—the sound of the ocean—when Ben said, "I got this e-mail yesterday, and I've been praying about it. I really don't want to share it with you, but I think I have to."

He then opened his phone and read the e-mail to me. An eleven-year-old boy named Garret had lost his mother to breast cancer three years earlier, and two days before, his father had passed away. Garret had Down Syndrome, and no other immediate family members were willing or able to take him. He would be placed into a state-controlled orphanage the following Wednesday. The e-mail ended by asking for prayers and a permanent home for the child.

My heart immediately started racing, and I had chills from head to toe. A month before I met Ben, I had had a vision that I was holding a child with Down Syndrome, and I heard God clearly say, "He is yours." The vision was so real that I immediately called my mom and my sister and told them about it. During our courtship, I told Ben that I was going to adopt a child with Down Syndrome one day. I asked him if he would be okay with that, and he said, "Sure...maybe." I'm positive that at the time he only said that because he wanted to marry me.

When Ben finished reading the e-mail to me that day at the beach, tears streamed down my face. He looked at me and said, "I knew it. I knew what you would say even before I shared it with you. I've been praying and praying, and I just don't know about this. We have four kids now. I'm out of town a lot. You teach children with various disabilities every day, and I'm afraid it would be too hard for you when you got home, too."

I listened to what he was saying, and I respected his words, but when he stopped talking, I immediately said, "Please, just keep praying."

The next morning, I went to the beach and spent time alone with God. I sat and thought of every logical reason why this child couldn't possibly be our son. As the ocean waves continually rolled onto the shoreline, I heard God's voice over and over, repeating, "He is yours. He is yours." In that moment, the Holy Spirit reminded me that Garret's mom had passed away three years ago. And it was three years ago when God had told me in my vision that "He is yours."

God had chosen me to be Garret's new mom. Out of everyone God could have chosen, He chose *me*.

I walked back to the beach house where Ben was drinking coffee on the back porch. With tears in my eyes, I looked at him and said, "God just reminded me that three years ago is when Garret's mom passed away, and it was three years ago that I had that vision. Can I call the social worker now?"

Ben nodded his head, smiled, and said, "Yes, go ahead and call."

Before I called, Ben and I asked our other four children their thoughts about Garret coming to live with us.

Our fourteen-year-old daughter immediately smiled and yelled, "Yes! Yes! Do it! Adopt him."

I told her that it wouldn't be that easy, and we needed to pray about it for a couple of days.

Her instant response kicked me in the stomach. "Mom, what is there to pray about? He is an orphan with no parents. The answer is clear."

Child-like faith—isn't it simply beautiful?

On Monday, I called the social worker. She explained that we couldn't be foster parents because we weren't in the foster system and hadn't completed the necessary requirements. However, we might be able to meet Garret's uncle who could potentially get legal custody and then allow us to keep Garret as "friends of the family." She gave me the uncle's phone number so that I could set up a meeting with him. I was so excited over the possibilities that I failed to fully understand the legal side of what the social worker was telling me.

Thinking that the uncle could grant us custody of Garret, I called him and told him we were interested in fostering Garret with the hopes of becoming his guardians. The uncle said he would be happy to meet with us the next day, so we ended our vacation early, packed up our beach bags, and headed back home to Birmingham, Alabama.

An hour before we were scheduled to meet Garret and his uncle on Tuesday, we received a phone call from the social worker.

"I cannot recommend in the court hearing tomorrow that Garret be placed with you because I've not met you or done a home visit," she said. "Garret's uncle cannot just give you custody. He would have to take custody and keep Garret while you and your husband go through foster classes."

I slowly realized that I hadn't paid close enough attention during my first conversation with the social worker. I explained that the uncle lived in California and that he couldn't keep Garret. However, the social worker responded that there was really no need for us to come to court in the morning. She wouldn't be able to speak with us any further.

I immediately started crying hysterically. We called an attorney and explained the situation. She advised that there was nothing we could do—Garret would have to go to the state orphanage until they found the right foster family.

I called my sister Michelle, and we prayed together. She reminded me that with faith all things are possible. In that moment, I knew that God was bigger than any court system. Ben and I decided that since God told us Garret would be our son, we would continue with our plans to meet him and his uncle, and we would still go to court the following morning to fight for him.

We met Garret for the first time on Tuesday, June 10, 2014, at 6:30 p.m. When Garret walked through the door, he gave Ben a big bear hug. Garret had Ben at "Hello!" After that night, Ben and I were both assured that God wanted Garret to live with us.

The next morning we went to court and sat with Garret and his uncle. Unbeknownst to us, the social worker and the guardian ad litem attorney for Garret watched us interact with him for about fifteen minutes. They asked to speak with us, and we briefly shared our hearts and intentions with them.

Despite what had been communicated to us the previous day, the social worker went on to recommend to the judge that we become Garret's legal custodial parents, with his uncle as a secondary custodial parent for whenever he's visiting Birmingham. The judge accepted the placement, and we all agreed with the terms of home visits for five months. At the end of those five months, we would all come back to court for final recommendations and placement.

On November 6, 2014, we went back to court, and my vision from more than three years before finally became a reality—Garret became a permanent member of our family!

And this is love: that we walk in obedience to his commands.
As you have heard from the beginning,
his command is that you walk in love. 2 John 6

A Surprise Sister

Jeanne Freeman

I'm embarrassed at what an ugly human being I was before I became a Christian. I had a lot of pride and hate in my heart. If someone rubbed me the wrong way, I decided that I didn't like them. I didn't need a real reason. Ever since I invited God into my life, however, He has changed me in so many ways.

For example, about a year after I became a Christian, I had some down time at work. I decided to catch up on my homework for a Bible study when I received an e-mail from my supervisor. To be brutally honest, I had no respect for her, and for years I had been very ugly to her. From the start of our working relationship, she was one of those people that rubbed me the wrong way. Even after becoming a Christian, I hadn't felt a need to change my behavior towards her. I began typing a nasty response to her and didn't really think twice about what or how I was communicating until I happened to look down at my homework. I was convicted by what I read:

"In the home, church, or workplace, has God ever called you to remain in a situation though you had lost respect for someone under whose authority God had placed you?"*

At that moment I knew God was speaking directly to me. I immediately changed my e-mail response to my supervisor and did what she asked me to do without any objections.

However, God wasn't done with me yet. My actions over the years toward my supervisor started weighing very heavily on my heart. I regretted how nasty I had been to her. There was no legitimate reason for my behavior. I called her to apologize, and during our conversation I found out that she was also a Christian. I believe that's why God worked on my heart about her—because she is my sister in Christ!

———**∿ .. ∿**———

Welcome with open arms fellow believers
who don't see things the way you do.
And don't jump all over them every time they do or say
something you don't agree with—even when it seems that
they are strong on opinions but weak in the faith department.
Remember, they have their own history to deal with. Treat them gently.
Romans 14:1 (MSG)

*Moore, Beth. *David: Seeking A Heart Like His.* Lifeway Press. 2010.

—— ᘉ‥ᘌ ——
Revealed Reflection Questions
—— ᘉ‥ᘌ ——

1. *An Unusual Dream* and *Bringing Garret Home* share the common thread of something having been revealed to them in a dream or vision. Can you describe a dream that you believe came from God?

    _____

    _____

    _____

    _____

2. Is God revealing Himself to you in a way that you can recognize? Maybe through a song, a friendship, or an unexpected message like Jeanne received through her Bible study in *A Surprise Sister*?

    _____

    _____

    _____

    _____

3. As stated in this section's introduction, God often makes a way for us long before we realize it. He sets things in motion days, weeks, or even years in advance. Can you identify an instance in your life where this has happened to you?

    _____

Question 3 continued

_____

_____

_____

4. Do you believe that God revealed Himself to us through the person Jesus Christ and continues to reveal Himself to us today through the Holy Spirit?

_____

_____

_____

_____

Challenge

Find a Bible verse where God revealed Himself through a dream. If you do not have a Bible, please refer to the Resources in the back of this book for online Bible options. We would love for you to share your verse and how it speaks to you on our Facebook page (www.facebook.com/GodIncidence) or Twitter account (@God_Incidence) using the hashtag #CoincidenceChallenge.

TRANSFORMED

Introduction to Transformed

Merriam-Webster dictionary defines the word *transformed* as:

a : to change in composition or structure *(inward)*
b : to change the outward form or appearance of
c : to change in character or condition

It's easy "to change in composition" or "to change the outward appearance" of something. A chef can add a few spices to a pot of tomato sauce and instantly change it from plain tomato sauce to chili sauce. A couple of gallons of paint and a few hours can remake a dull room into a bright, cheerful gathering place. A visit to the salon can transform an outdated hairstyle into something modern. We relate to these examples because we've all either had firsthand experience with them or watched someone else make similar changes.

Often when we make a decision to change something, we expect to see immediate results, like we might see with a new hairstyle. Sometimes, however, the transformation is more of a process than a simple procedure. For example, we can decide to change something, like a character trait, that isn't outward or superficial. Those types of changes aren't nearly as easy as changing something simple. They take time, prayer, and a lot of patience.

Establishing a relationship with God is another area that can take time. You didn't get to know your best friend overnight, did you? That friendship took time and nurturing to mature. A relationship with God is the same way. God doesn't force Himself upon us. He gives us a free will so that we have the option to choose His transformation or to follow a different path. The choice is ours. Be aware that when you first start to allow God to transform your life, you may not see immediate results.

Sometimes, however, God changes a person so dramatically that it appears almost unbelievable. The Bible contains the story of Saul's conversion in the book of Acts. Who was this man Saul? He was a person who relentlessly persecuted and killed believers in God. He went door to door searching for Christians, men or women, and dragging them off to prison for their beliefs. He even approved of the massacring of Christian teachers. Then in Acts 9, we find Saul traveling on the road to Damascus, a town where he planned to conduct more raids. A bright light suddenly appeared on the road, blinding him. In the moments that followed, God changed Saul's name and transformed Saul's heart and life. Paul, as he would now be known, went from being a murdering Christian-hater to a man who would become one of the most influential evangelists in history. He would later die as a martyr for his faith. Can you imagine how unbelievable it must have seemed to those early Christians that the man they had known as Saul was now a changed man? Surely, such a drastic change couldn't happen so rapidly, but it did. This story proves that God doesn't judge us by our past. Paul says in 1 Timothy 1:13, "Even though I was once a blasphemer and a persecutor and a violent man, I was shown mercy because I acted in ignorance and unbelief."

This next section of stories illustrates how real and powerful God's transformations can be in today's world. These are not just "once upon a time" stories—they are real-world, everyday happenings. You will see how a high school boy's brave testimony changed the course of a family's trajectory in *Full Circle* and how a sister's long-time prayer for her brother's life resulted in a modern-day Saul-to-Paul conversion in *4:59*. Just in case those stories aren't persuasive enough, *Victim to Victor* reveals how an abused, drug-addicted young woman became a missionary.

Giving in and allowing God to take over your life benefits more than just you. If you allow God to control the helm of your life and orchestrate the details, He will transform you in ways that you can't even imagine.

4:59

Brian Levering

I was a sold-out atheist for twenty years of my life.

When I was sixteen years old, I became friends with a guy named Sheldon, and he's the one who convinced me that God didn't exist. Before that, I was kind of agnostic. My parents never took me or my siblings to church, so I guess I sort of believed in God only because I had never thought about anything else. Then I met Sheldon, and he convinced me that the evidence for evolution was true, which made sense to me at the time.

I'm a pretty intellectual person, so I began reading books that helped encourage my atheism. Then I began arguing for atheism. I was trying to convert people away from Christianity—I was literally waging war against God. I wasn't a violent, resistant, or antagonistic atheist. I didn't feel like Christians were evil and needed to be erased from every part of our society. I just believed that Christians were wrong and I was right.

My sister, on the other hand, was a sold-out follower of Christ and a published Bible study author. At times, I would actually try to talk her out of her faith. She never shunned me for it; she would just bring me closer and love on me all the more. Even though she didn't have the fundamental answers I was looking for, she would lovingly engage in debate, and she always pointed me back to the love of God and faith in Jesus as the only source for my answers. We never fought about our differing beliefs—we just didn't agree. Little did I know that she was praying every day that God would reveal Himself to me, somehow, in some way.

At age nineteen I started my career in the music industry. I was a singer/songwriter experiencing everything that type of life entails—sex, drugs, and rock & roll. Yet, God was at work. The night my oldest son was born, God began to answer my sister's prayers. Something took place inside of me that made me begin to question if God might actually exist. The moment I laid eyes on my son, I felt a love that seemed supernatural. I didn't understand how I could automatically have that kind of love for something the moment I saw it. The experience compelled me to start attending church for the first time in my life at twenty-seven years old. I attended a small church for about six months, but it wasn't long before the desire faded away. However, from that point on, even though I still claimed to be an atheist, a part of me was curious and I started searching for something more in life.

In 2008, when I was thirty-six years old, my sister invited me to a Christmas play at her church because my niece was performing in it. I went solely because I wanted to see my niece. What I saw when I attended was the contemporary church, which until that point I didn't know existed. I thought all churches were like the traditional churches I had sporadically attended in the past. The worship band and the Christian rock music that they played were actually pretty good, and I thought it was pretty cool. The church was starting a six-week series titled "The Bucket List." I had just seen the movie of the same name the week before, and I thought the series sounded pretty interesting, so I committed to attending for six weeks. By the third and fourth weeks of the series, I was really excited about going back to church and would look forward to it all week.

During the same six weeks, I also started listening exclusively to Christian radio. My sister gave me books on Christianity and faith, and I was reading things I had never read before. At this point, I was seeking for the sole purpose of giving Christianity a "day in court." I enjoyed attending church, the people were pretty cool, and they were really accepting and nice. I say that because every Sunday when I attended I was extremely hung over from the night before. I played a lot of gigs on Saturday nights, and although I'm sure I reeked of liquor and cigarettes, everyone was really welcoming.

When the six weeks were over, I continued to attend. I felt encouraged, and every week it felt like a reset button had been hit. I was becoming more and more interested. Each Sunday after church we had a family lunch at my sister's house, and it was a fun routine. I was doing what I think a lot of people do—going to church on Sunday and doing the other six days on my own.

After about four months, I really gave some thought to what all of this meant for me. If God was real and what they were preaching about was authentic, I wanted it. However, being a Christian had to be more than just going to church, saying the prayer to accept Christ, and reading the Bible and other books. I thought there needed to be a recognizable change in my life, and at that point I just didn't feel any different. I was doing the "right things," but nothing was happening. I had reached a crossroads. In the back of my head, I heard God telling me, "You've always been a fighter. You've had to fight for everything you've ever had in life, so if you really want this, you need to fight for it." I confided in my sister, and her advice was to keep fighting, keep seeking God, and eventually He would show Himself to me. My response to her was "I'm going to keep searching. I'm going to keep going until I get to the bottom of this thing."

That conversation with my sister happened on a Thursday, and the following day my friend Anthony reached out to me. I hadn't heard from him in two years. He and I had done business together for many years in the past, even traveling internationally together. He contacted me via e-mail and said, "Hey man, I really wanna get together with you. I want to talk with you about what's been going on in my life."

So, I asked him what he was talking about, and he told me he had found Jesus.

I said to him, "Man, that's crazy because I've been on this journey of searching for this thing... this is nuts!"

Initially, I didn't think I could see Anthony any earlier than six weeks out because of my work schedule. He said that would be fine, but then I was overcome by this sense of urgency. I called him and told him I had to see him that day. So I cleared my schedule and called my wife to tell her we were making the hour and a half drive to see Anthony that night.

When I first met Anthony years before, he was an incredibly ruthless businessman. He would cut a man's throat for a nickel, and that's what I loved about him. He was also a hard-core drug addict. When I walked into his house that Friday night, I saw crosses everywhere, and as soon as he began to talk, I knew he was a changed man. He looked the same, but something different shone in his eyes. As he began to speak, his voice had a softness that had never been there before. He shared his testimony with me and my wife, and it was powerful as he described the night God reached down out of nowhere to rescue him.

Anthony had been sitting in his living room when all of a sudden a tingling came over his head. It went through his face, into his shoulders, and down his chest. He was sweating profusely, and he thought that he was dying. All he could think to do was grab his family and go to the floor in prayer. He prayed, "Lord, if I'm dying, just take care of my family." His family called the ambulance, and he was transported to the hospital, where he spent four days undergoing tests. The doctors couldn't find anything wrong with him, but he knew exactly what had happened—God touched his life and changed him. He knew it beyond the shadow of a doubt.

When Anthony returned home from the hospital, he was completely changed. He called his drug dealers and told them, "I'm a different person. God changed my life, and if you ever want to hear about Jesus, call me. Otherwise, lose my phone number."

He had been delivered from multiple addictions—cocaine, alcohol, and cigarettes. He had previously smoked four packs a day. Overnight, the addictions were gone.

As Anthony told me his story, he wept. I looked at him and thought about how unbelievable it was. This was the type of change that I had just been talking about with my sister the day before. Anthony's testimony rocked my world. It showed me the reality of God's love, power, and grace. Anthony was a completely different person, and I wanted what he had.

Then Anthony told me the other reason he had reached out to me. Over the last few days, at exactly 4:59 a.m. each day, he would wake up out of a sound sleep with me on his mind. At first he blew it off, but when the same thing kept happening every morning at the same time, he realized that he needed to reach out to me.

As my family and I were leaving his house that night, Anthony gave me a book to read that talked about the listening prayer—a prayer to hear God's voice speaking to you. When we arrived home, I poured myself a couple of glasses of vodka and pineapple juice—or whatever I was drinking at the time—and I read the book. I stayed up reading until probably one o'clock in the morning. Then I actually kneeled down beside my bed and prayed the listening prayer before I went to sleep.

That night, I dreamed I was in this weird complex of some sort, and I was looking at a person painting a mural of a face. Then I flashed from one place to another, as dreams do, and I was driving a car with Anthony in the passenger seat. He spoke to me, from the position of God, and said, "Man, I could do this for you. I can paint you brand new, but I don't feel a sense of urgency in you. I need to know—do you really want this?"

Before I could answer the question, a big, black snake fell across my shoulders. I wasn't startled by it. I remember the snake's head was all the way down on the floorboard to my left, and his tail was all the way down where the stick shift was on my right. The only thing I could think was "How am I gonna get this snake off my shoulders?"

At that moment, I was startled awake by a loud, thunderous voice in my room that said, "Scrolls!" I literally thought someone had broken into my house and was standing in my room. After I scoured the room with my eyes to make sure I wasn't about to be killed, I looked at the clock to see what time it was. I didn't know exactly what had happened, but I had a sense that it was pretty important. I immediately got out of bed and began writing down everything about the dream.

When I finished writing, it hit me that the clock had read exactly 4:59 the moment I woke up. It felt like I was in a movie as the memory hit me—the memory of Anthony telling me how God had spoken to him about me at 4:59 in the morning. And then I knew that God had actually spoken to me. It was a divine intervention. 4:59 meant something, and I knew God had woken me up at 4:59 so He could show me that this dream was no accident. I lay in bed that Saturday morning with tears in my eyes, and for the first time, I gave my life to Christ. This time, it was for real.

For my gig later that night, I decided that I needed to wear a Christian shirt, so I went out and bought one that said "crucified" on it with a big picture of Jesus on the cross. I wore it on stage that night. A few hundred people were at the bar, and I stood up in the middle of it all and told people that I had given my life to Christ. I was witnessing to the people about what God had done and that God was real. I knew I was going to be an evangelist right from the beginning. That Saturday night was the first night I didn't have a drink in almost ten years.

The next day I went to church with my family. Afterward, we went back to my sister's house for lunch, just like we always did. But that Sunday was different. As we sat around the table, my wife said, "Why don't you tell them about the dream you had on Friday night?"

I proceeded to do so, and when I got to the part about the snake falling on my shoulders, I felt this power come over me. It was coming down from above the right side of my body, and I lost all control. It felt like I began to explode. I started crying and weeping, and I actually felt the darkness that had gripped my life leave my body. I had my head down for what felt like ten minutes. When I picked my head up, everything looked different. I had given my life to Christ on Saturday, but I clearly felt the presence of the Holy Spirit on Sunday.

I've never been the same since that day. I saw things clearly for the first time—it was like colors were different. I could hear things for the first time—profanity that I had spoken so casually before now seemed to pierce my ears. In that one moment, I was redeemed and delivered from a lifelong addiction to alcohol that I had been powerless against on my own.

I remember looking right at my sister and saying, "God spoke to me. God spoke to me!"

My sister and brother-in-law wept with me because they knew exactly what had happened to me. They had been praying for it for years. I couldn't fully grasp it at the time, but they had witnessed a miracle.

What was so incredibly powerful about this whole experience was that God not only fixed in me what I knew was broken, but He also fixed problems I didn't know I had, like my foul language. The way I viewed things was different too. I remember shortly after that Sunday, a guy came into my office and flashed a pornographic picture in front of my face. Before I could even think, I reacted. Where I previously would have entertained the photo, I now recoiled as soon as he put it in front of me. I hadn't been taught to do this—my body was now reacting to the very nature of the Holy Spirit that had been given to me.

The thing I'm most thankful for is that Jesus didn't just save me; He saved my whole family. He changed the direction of my kids' lives forever. The sins of the father will be visited on the son no more! It wasn't until a few days, maybe even a week later, that I realized why 4:59 was so important. The Sunday that I first knew the Holy Spirit was with me was April 5, 2009 … 4/5/9 … 4:59.

At once the man was cured; he picked up his mat and walked.
The day on which this took place was the Sabbath (Sunday). John 5:9

The verse above, John 5:9, can be closely related to Brian's experience. It is interesting to note that John is the 4th gospel and the reference is in the 5th chapter and the 9th verse — 4-5-9.

Connect With The Contributing Author

Brian is a Spirit-led evangelist.
E-mail: healingpower459@yahoo.com

The Biggest Loser...Ever

Danny Cahill

In December 2007, my life was in a tailspin, and my weight was at an all-time high of 460 pounds. I had overcome a gambling addiction and was working hard to pay off the debt that I had racked up, but the stress of the debt and the concern over my weight was taking a toll on my family. I hated my job, and I was angry all of the time. Years before, I had followed the "safe" path and worked a steady job to support my family instead of pursuing my passion and dreams of playing music.

My wife Darci, who dealt with her own physical struggles as well as depression, found refuge in a small group of women. These women prayed with her, supported her, and encouraged her. It was in this small group that someone asked Darci if we had ever seen a television show called *The Biggest Loser*. They described the show as a competition that helped obese people lose weight and change their lives. Not long after they talked about the show, a new girl came to the meeting. This girl came up to Darci and said, "There's getting ready to be an event in your life, and God is going to change everything. He's going to bless you beyond measure. The blessings are going to come so quickly, it will overwhelm you." Darci had no idea what this girl was talking about, but figured God would reveal it in His own time.

Around that same time I found Darci and my daughter Mary watching *The Biggest Loser* on television. I yelled at them to turn it off because I thought it was a show designed to make fun of obese people. The following week when it came on, I sat down with Darci and watched a little bit of the episode.

"Man, I'm an athletic guy for my size. I think I could do that!" I said to Darci. "I played football, and I think I would be good on that show! And you know what? I haven't felt challenged in years. That's what I need—a challenge!"

When I mentioned my interest in *The Biggest Loser*, Darci knew that *this* was what the "new" girl had been talking about.

In addition to her prayer group, Darci was also attending personal development seminars on the weekends. She had expressed an interest in having me attend, but I wanted no part of it. I didn't have the time, energy, or desire to give up three weekends of my life to attend one of those seminars.

After Darci's first weekend, I saw such a change in her. She was happier, and she was on the road to making healthy lifestyle changes. Her relationship with God began to flourish. All of her changes only served to show how far apart we were growing, and I knew I needed to do something. I finally reached the point where I realized that if I wanted to preserve my marriage, I had to attend one of the seminars.

I went to the men's weekend seminar, and everything was okay until we got to an exercise where each person in the group had to be physically held up by the others in the group. When I saw my group holding up the first person, I wanted to disappear. I went from person to person saying, "You don't have to hold me up. It's okay. We can skip me."

The head of the seminar said to me, "Are you crazy? We can hold you up buddy!"

And they did. They held me up while a song played that said you can always start again tomorrow. That experience had a profound effect on me. It showed me that there was no shame in getting help. I didn't have to do everything by myself. No matter how big my problem, there were others who could, and would, help me.

For the first time I was also able to see how I had been treating my family. I would lose my temper and fail to consider their feelings or desires because I was so wrapped up in myself and my daily struggle of trying to prove that I could do everything on my own. Instead of loving and nurturing my family, I blamed them for all of the work I had to do.

I came home from the seminar wanting to be a different husband and father but found that it was hard work. I knew I had a long way to go, but I was encouraged when my children told me that I was a better dad and was yelling a lot less. Darci told me she felt like I was once again the joyful, passionate man she had fallen in love with. Their encouragement and support gave me the determination to attend the other two weekends of the seminar.

During my second weekend I wrote in my journal:
What to do to achieve my dreams:
1. Live my contract: "I am a joyful and passionate man!"
2. Lose the weight!
3. Lose the debt.
(2 and 3 can be achieved by winning The Biggest Loser!)
[signed] Charles D. Cahill
July 19, 2008

By the end of that weekend, I had declared to everyone that "I'm going to get on that show *[The Biggest Loser]* and win it! I believe it is my destiny."

When I got home and shared my decision with Darci, she was thrilled. My decision was an answer to her prayers.

The next time Darci met with her prayer group, she shared the news that I was going to try to get on *The Biggest Loser*. The same "new girl" said, "He's going to win that show. He won't get on the first time he tries, but he's going to win it when he does."

I filled out the application with only one week left to submit it. I rushed to make my audition video and mail everything by the deadline. I wanted to be a part of Season 6, but I didn't have a lot of confidence. I soon found out that Season 6 had already been cast, so I set my sights on Season 7. Since Season 7 was *The Biggest Loser: Families,* I auditioned with my sister Charla. We took off from work and stood in line for hours at a casting call in Oklahoma City. Finally, we were brought in for an interview, and it went really well. A few days later we received a call back for a second interview, all the while sensing how surreal this whole process felt. We did well on the second interview, and I wondered if this was it.

People from the show called several times and asked for more information. I tried out again with two different friends from church, and I was asked if there were any other family members that might try out with me. At that point I knew the show was really interested in me, and I begged some other family members to audition with me, but they were all too embarrassed to take their shirts off in front of millions of people. It was so frustrating! Finally, Darci and I decided to make a video together and apply.

We were really excited when I received word to expect a call before a certain date if we had been cast for the show. That date came and went, but there was no phone call. I was devastated. For a while, I stopped watching the show and would have nothing to do with it. Eventually, my anger subsided, and I watched Season 7.

Then an old friend tagged me in a photo on Facebook. In the picture I was seventeen years old, in great shape, wearing a muscle shirt, and playing in a band. I showed the photo to a coworker and asked, "Why am I not playing music and performing? Why am I sitting here in this office and doing something I never really wanted to do, something I settled for? Why am I here?"

"I think you are the only one who can answer that," my coworker answered. "Why are you?"

His reply hit me like a ton of bricks! The answer to all of those desires was to win *The Biggest Loser*. I posted a comment on that photo stating "I want that body back! I'm trying out for *The Biggest Loser!*"

That night I went home and printed out another application. I made several copies because no matter how many times it took, I was going to get on that show. I sent in another video and then heard about another casting call in Oklahoma City. This time it said applicants could come with or without a partner. I told Darci, "This is it! Last time I think my problem might have been my partners, but this is a singles' season. I'm going to do this thing!"

I managed to get a VIP pass at the casting call and moved to the front of the line. I walked into the interview and sat at a table with other applicants. The interviewer told us that they had to see almost a thousand people that day, so we each had sixty seconds to show him who we were and to make a memorable impression.

The first person who went was boring, the second was dull, and the third was almost crazy. When my turn came, I knew I had to be big in more ways than just my physical size. I slammed my hand on the table, and as loud as I could, I yelled, "Hi! I'm Danny Cahill, and I am the next Biggest Loser! In fact, when you put me on the show, you're going to have cast the Biggest Loser ever. I have absolutely no doubt that I will lose over 200 pounds! I was born for this!"

I went on for over two minutes, and no one could stop me. The people at the other table in the room stopped talking and were looking at me, too. I knew I only had a few more seconds left to say something that would do more than shock them with my volume, so I continued, "And I'm tired of being on bottom! I want to be on top again!"

Everyone, including the other hopefuls, burst out laughing. They all knew the double meaning— tired of being on the bottom of life, but also being on the bottom during sex with my wife. Good or bad, I knew that the casting people weren't going to forget me.

I knew I had done what was necessary to make a memorable impression. I felt like celebrating, so I met Darci and our family for ribs and beer. I told them, "There is no way I am not getting an interview. If they don't remember me, something is seriously wrong."

I got called back for a second interview. While driving down to Oklahoma City, I knew crying would be effective in this meeting. I tried to think of the most heart-breaking things to make myself cry. I managed to squeeze out one tear. Crying during the interview was going to be tougher than I realized.

When the interview started, I was screaming on the inside "I've gotta cry" but nothing seemed to move me. Then the interviewers asked how my weight had affected my life. In a split second I thought of the physical pain and the fear of disease and death. I thought of my inability to be the husband and father I knew I could be. I thought of the embarrassment, the shame, the hurt, the anger, and the depression I had endured over the years. I thought of the disappointment to everyone around me and, most importantly, to myself. All of a sudden, I burst into tears. The tears continued throughout my interview and all the way home. As I cried, I realized how much had been bottled up inside of me for years. My pride had not allowed me to reach out for help or to even recognize how much hurt I felt. I always had to be the guy who held it all together—until that interview. Then I started laughing because no matter how much I had tried to hide it, it was very obvious by my weight that I was the guy who *didn't* have it all together.

Darci and the kids were so excited when I returned home and told them about the interview. Our family and friends were praying and believing that the time was right. Over the next few months, I was inundated with phone calls and requests from the show. It was taking up so much of our time that it actually became annoying. Darci and I wondered if we were being tested to see if we were really serious. We knew that if I was chosen to be on the show, the entire family would be affected. I would have to drop everything to do it, and my family would have to support me in it.

It was the end of April 2009, and I hadn't heard anything lately from the casting department. Darci and I were trying to trust God, but we were frustrated. One day at work, I looked at that photo on Facebook again, and I began to weep. I had a fear in the pit of my stomach that I hadn't made it again. I prayed, "God, why do You do this to me? You gave me this desire and now You put me through this disappointment? You say You aren't a liar, that Your word is true. Then why are You doing this to me?"

I felt compelled to open my Bible at that moment, so I took it out and placed it on my desk. It seemed to open naturally to Genesis 50:20— "You intended to harm me, but God intended it for good to accomplish what is now being done, the saving of many lives." I began to cry, and I immediately called Darci. I told her that I was going to be on the show. She asked me if *The Biggest Loser* had called. I told her no but that God had told me I was going to be on the show. I then explained to her what had happened. I finished with "I believe my being on that show is going to change millions of lives."

A few days later I got the call that I would be going to Los Angeles for more interviews and tests. I took vacation time from work, went shopping with Darci for some nice clothes, and shot video all week in preparation for the trip.

The plane ride to Los Angeles was uneventful but embarrassing. Two seats had to be bought for me, and I had to use a seat belt extender. When I arrived, I got my three bags and headed for the shuttle that would take me where I needed to go. As I climbed on, I said, "I've got more luggage than a woman."

"Watch it, buddy!" a large woman replied while laughing.

I liked her immediately, but when I noticed she was carrying a notebook with *The Biggest Loser* symbol on it, I panicked. I was worried that I wasn't supposed to talk to any of the other possible contestants, so I ignored her.

When we got off the shuttle together, she asked, "Are you here for the—"

"Yes! And you need to stand over there and me over here. We shouldn't talk to each other."

She looked at me and started laughing so hard that I couldn't miss how hilarious I had sounded. After that we hit it off and chatted all the way to the hotel. Little did I know that Liz would later end up being one of my best friends on the show. Once we arrived at the hotel, we went to our rooms, and we weren't able to go anywhere without an escort.

While in the hotel, I took test after test and filled out all kinds of paperwork. It was three days before I had an interview. They asked me, "Danny, you said that you used to hide in the closet and eat an entire can of cake frosting, then feel ashamed. Why didn't you just stop?"

I tried to come up with a profound analysis, but I came away wondering if I had blown the entire interview. To my relief, I was called to another interview. I felt like I had one last chance to make a lasting impact, so I looked at the man who had asked me about eating the cake frosting and said, "You asked me the other day why I didn't just stop. If I knew that, I wouldn't be sitting here!" Then I broke down and said, "I am begging you. Don't send me back to my two-job, bill-paying, cesspool of a life; because if you do, I will put me back on a shelf and say, 'I'll take care of you later,' like I have for the past fifteen years. My daughter and my son and my wife are counting on me, and I don't want to die!"

Everyone was silent. The interview ended, and I returned to my hotel room. I called Darci and told her that I had just hit a home run, knocked it right out of the park. Later that day I left for home and was told I would hear from the casting people in a week. I didn't like leaving Los Angeles without knowing if I had made the show or not—it scared me. When I got home, I channeled all of my nervous energy into filming every minute of my life.

I planned a party for the day I expected to hear from *The Biggest Loser*. Over one hundred of our family and friends gathered with us at a restaurant while we waited for the call.

"There's no way they aren't going to put you on the show!" Darci said.

I was grateful for her confidence, but I wasn't so sure. When the call came in, I turned on my speakerphone, but it was cutting in and out, so I had to put the phone to my ear. I heard the news and yelled, "I'm going!" My loved ones were ecstatic, and it didn't take long for news to travel. Soon all hopes of confidentiality were out the window.

On Mother's Day 2009, Darci and the kids drove me to the airport to embark on my journey. After I went through security, I turned around and waved until I was out of sight. I had no idea when I would be back. As hard as the separation would be, we all hoped it would be a long time before I saw them again. I was able to pre-board the flight because of my size, and I had two seats again. I asked the flight attendant to film me, and she did. I wanted a record of just how big I was on my last plane trip at over 400 pounds.

Once I arrived, the first official weigh-in was held, and Season 8 would begin the next day. When I weighed in at 430 pounds, I was dismayed to find out that I had already lost 30 pounds before the show had even started. My goal was to lose as much as possible to win. I immediately got on a treadmill and felt proud that I could jog four of the twenty minutes that I was on it. Then I went outside and walked up a very steep hill twice, which was extremely hard. For a while I played one-on-one basketball with a guy named Thai, who beat me mercilessly. Afterwards, I returned to my hotel room. To me, the game was on the moment I weighed in. No more eating junk food; it was time to lose the weight and get healthy. I measured out my hotel room and walked back and forth for a total of 1-1/4 miles while watching the Season 7 finale. Exhausted, I laid down and fell asleep... and missed the end of the show. I didn't know who won Season 7 until the next morning.

All too soon it was time to head to *The Biggest Loser* ranch, and that was pretty frightening. The mansion where we stayed was awesome, but the reality of what was about to happen started to sink in, and I knew it was really time to focus on the task. When I arrived, I didn't say much to anyone; I just wanted to observe and size up my competition. I missed my family terribly, and when I handed over my cell phone, I realized I would possibly have no contact with them until I arrived home again, whenever that would be.

I knew what to expect from watching previous seasons on television. Or at least I thought I did. That first day of workouts went on for hours. I thought that the twenty minutes on the treadmill at the hotel the previous day was a huge victory. Bob Harper and Jillian Michaels put the contestants on treadmills while waiting for the individual training sessions. I was on the treadmill for over an hour before I was even called!

When Bob dismissed everyone for lunch, he held me back and made me work out even longer. I was exhausted, and I hurt all over. At one point, I sat down on a bench and slid off of it to the ground. If you watch episode one of Season 8, you'll see Bob lean over and say to me, "I'm never going to let you rest because I have no idea how long you're going to be here. Whether you go home the first week or last the entire season, every day I'm going to make you feel like you're going home tomorrow. Now, get up." And the workout continued.

At one point during that extended workout, Bob asked me, "What happened to you?"

"I just gave up. Fifteen years ago, I gave up on music. I gave up on my joy. And I just gave up on me."

"So you've spent the last fifteen years taking care of everyone else and rejecting yourself?"

In that moment, the light bulb went on for me. I finally realized that it wasn't anyone else that had rejected me, not my family, not my friends—it was *me* who had rejected me. I alone was at fault for rejecting who I was and what I desired to do with my life.

Bob continued on, "Now I'm going to be 'your Danny.' Now I'm going to take care of you."

That day, I realized that in serving God all those years, I had merely gone through the motions, begrudgingly doing what I believed I had to do. I never thought God would or should take care of me. Deep down, I never really believed that God loved me and wanted me to be happy, so I took control of everything in my life instead of trusting in God. For the first time, I really saw myself through my Heavenly Father's eyes, and truly understood His love for me, as His child. I reached out to God in a whole new way that day.

My new relationship with God cleared the path for me to get through that first workout, and then the next workout, and the next. In the days following that first workout with Bob, I thought of all the bad decisions I had made by living a life of blaming others, and even God, for my circumstances. I made a list of all my wrong decisions—what I should have done but didn't, and what I shouldn't have done but did. For the first time in my life, I started taking responsibility for my actions in a healthy way. I repented to God for my self-destructive and rebellious behavior.

At every turn, I saw new possibilities for my life. Every morning I would wake up and go to the little wicker basket my mother-in-law had hidden in my suitcase. In the basket were a hundred cards, each with a verse of scripture or words of encouragement written on it. I never ceased to be amazed how each day's card related to what I was feeling and going through. On challenge days, it was uncanny how the morning's verse directly related to the challenge.

I didn't go to the ranch to preach Jesus to people, but I did have a deep desire to *be Jesus* to people. I wanted to win, but I didn't want to destroy my competitors in doing so. I was determined to win with love and compassion. Knowing how much God loved me made it easier to love others, especially when tempers flared.

I don't know what everyone else's workout regimens were like, but I know that I averaged between seven and nine hours every day. At night I would lie in bed, physically, emotionally, and mentally spent, and think about my family. I worried that they were okay without me and without my salary because I had taken a leave of absence from my job to be on the show. I missed my wife and kids terribly.

One night during week five, I woke up at two o'clock in the morning to get some water. I was desperately missing my family, so right then and there, I started writing them a letter. In the letter I penned the words to the song "My Wish" by Rascal Flatts. I was crying so hard that my tears were wetting the paper. The next morning I mailed the letter to my family.

That same week, I lost a challenge where the prize was a video from our families. I was devastated. My closest friend on the show, Liz, who was also the woman I rode the shuttle with, asked if I would like to watch her video with her. I agreed, thinking that I might at least get to share her joy. But when the video started, I realized that Liz had given up her family video so that I could see my family! But what was even more amazing than her generosity was what my family said to me on the video. My wife and kids recited the words to *My Wish* by Rascal Flatts!

My letter and Darci's video crossed in the mail, but it was not a coincidence that both contained the same message. God had been directing both pieces of mail. I felt honored that in all the years of suffering through my selfishness, temper, and neglect, my wife had never stopped believing in me and praying for what was best for me. I knew at that moment that I had the greatest wife in the world.

Through supernatural events and divine intervention—and the hard work I continued to put in at the gym—I made it through all of the eliminations and to the final four. My dear friend Liz made it through, along with Amanda, who I had also become close with, and Rudy.

Through every workout, every challenge, and every moment of missing my family, I worked with every fiber of my being to win *The Biggest Loser,* and I did! To this day, I am still the biggest male loser the show has ever seen, losing a total of 239 pounds and 55.8 percent of my body weight.

I've been brought back to the show several times to inspire other contestants. I've been on a number of talk shows, and I've been blessed with the opportunity to speak at motivational events for businesses and organizations. I also speak in churches where I am able to freely share my faith. I know that it was God's will for me to win the show because it has given me the opportunity to minister to others and to speak about how amazing our God is.

*You intended to harm me, but God intended it for good
to accomplish what is now being done, the saving of many lives.*
Genesis 50:20

Story adapted from *Losing Big: The Incredible Untold Story of Danny & Darci Cahill.*
Published by Harrison House Publishers, Tulsa, OK. 2012. Used with permission.

Connect With The Contributing Author

Danny and Darci are the Connect Group Pastors at The Bridge
in Bixby, OK (www.thebridgebixby.com). Danny has also
created and facilitates The Journey Training
(www.thejourneytraining.com).
Website: www.thedannycahill.com
E-mail: danny@thedannycahill.com
facebook.com/loseyourquit
facebook.com/thedannycahill
Twitter and Instagram: @dannycahill1

Full Circle

Jamie Santos

As a young Christian guy on fire for God, I had an opportunity to talk about my faith in my high school classroom one day. My teacher gave me permission to share the gospel message in class.

As I was speaking to my classmates, a girl jumped up and began cursing me out from head to toe. I tried not to pay much attention to her, but she continued cursing me the whole time I was trying to talk about Jesus. By the time I finished, I felt like God had let me down. I was so upset that I ran out of class, left school, and ended up getting suspended for two days. After the suspension ended, I really didn't give the incident or the girl much thought.

Years later I was playing in a church softball game when I noticed a girl watching me and winking at me from the other team's bench. I figured I must have looked pretty good that day to warrant the attention. Later, as she walked over to me, I thought to myself, "Hey, I think she likes me. All right, the game is on!"

As she neared me, she looked me in the face and said, "You don't know who I am, Jamie."

"I've no idea," I said, "but I would like to meet you."

Then she started crying!

"What's the matter?" I asked. "Did I offend you? Did I hurt you?" In my head I was thinking about all the things I'd done in the past that could have caused this outburst of tears.

Then she responded, "I'm the girl that was in your high school class."

Instantly, my mind flashed back to that day, and I remembered that when she had been cursing me, God spoke to me. In a moment of boldness, before I ran out of the classroom, I said to her, "If you come to God today, you're gonna be saved. Your mom's gonna be saved. Your dad, your brother, everybody in your family—they're all going to be completely saved by God in days to come."

I had forgotten all about what I'd said to her! But she never did. She told me she went home that night, cried with her mom, and told her mom what I had said. She and her mom received the Lord right then and there. Four years later, her dad received the Lord. Her brother is now a missionary.

That day on the softball field, I thought she was checking me out, but it had nothing to do with me. God brought us back together through a church softball game so she could share with me what He had done for her family.

But you will receive power when the Holy Spirit comes on you;
and you will be my witnesses in Jerusalem, and in all Judea and
Samaria, and to the ends of the earth. Acts 1:8

Victim to Victor

Rayna Cohen

I grew up in a home with a Catholic parent and a Jewish parent, but we never practiced either of those faiths. The only time I was exposed to religion was when I stayed the night at a girlfriend's house and her family would take me to church in the morning. I would spend most of the service thinking about what I would eat for breakfast when we went out after church. I thought church was a chore, and I hated going.

I was a junior in high school when my parents split up. After their divorce, I started dating a boy named Dave, and we partied together all the time. When I was about seventeen years old, I moved in with Dave as a show of rebellion against my family. I entered into the hippie scene of peace and karma. I rebelled against religion and considered myself an atheist. I bashed God and considered people who believed in Him to be weak. I bad-mouthed Christians and thought to myself, "Why do you need God when you can accomplish anything on your own?" I knew my way was right, and I wouldn't be convinced otherwise.

After Dave and I moved in together, he started physically and emotionally abusing me. He called me names and threatened to hurt my family if I ever told anyone that he hit me. He made me believe that it was all my fault. One day I left the apartment and failed to do something that he had asked me to do. When I returned home, he swung his elbow at me in anger and split my eye open before I even realized what was happening. (I still have a scar from that incident.) He didn't want anyone to know what he did to me, so he forbade me from leaving the apartment.

By the time I turned eighteen, Dave and I started doing prescription pills, Oxycodone and Xanax. The pills had been prescribed to me after an accident I had in high school, but because of my situation, I took them all the time. The pills became my crutch. I didn't feel sad when I was on them. Actually, I didn't feel anything—I was numb physically and emotionally. My parents told me that I needed to get off the pills, but I was eighteen and told them that the doctors had prescribed the pills for me and that I didn't have to listen to their opinions.

Dave and I lived off of my college loans because he refused to get a job. He spent my loan money on useless things, so we hit rock bottom when I ran out of money. As a result, we faced eviction from our home. I told him that we each needed to go back to living with our parents. I promised him that even though we would be living separately, we would still stay together. However, in my mind, I had already left Dave and his abusive behavior. I had been searching for a way out, and here it was. The eviction was a blessing in disguise, enabling me to finally break free. I remember texting him as soon as I moved out—"It's done. It's over."

Even though our breakup had brought freedom, I didn't want to be living back home. I felt like I had taken a step backwards, which led me into a depression. I was still using narcotics, Xanax, and maybe Vicodin. (I think I was on Vicodin, but I really don't remember because Vicodin can change how a person thinks.) I do remember moving back to my dad's house and thinking, "I don't want to be here."

I started dating another guy right away. He was ten years older than me and had his life together. I thought this new relationship was the perfect opportunity for me to move out again. Since I was selfish, I pretended to love my new boyfriend just so I could move into his house. After I moved in, depression hit hard because I realized that I was using him. I knew that I was wrong, but I was so addicted to the drugs that I didn't know how to get out of the situation. It wasn't long before I found out that my boyfriend was cheating on me, and I moved back in with my dad.

That's when I decided I wanted to get clean. I went through an in-home rehab in the fall of 2010. I was clean for about five months, but I relapsed in March 2011. At the time, my dad and I fought constantly, so I moved in with my mom. I started attending church with her to make her happy.

I tried to give the illusion that I was a perfect person by going to church while also hoping that my mom wouldn't notice how bad my addiction was becoming again. Two months after my relapse, I decided to go back on the treatments for addiction.

Unfortunately, I still hadn't changed my friends, and I met another guy who got me in a lot of trouble. He stole a gun from my mom's house and committed two armed home invasions with that gun. When the police traced him and the gun back to my mom's house, they assumed I was involved as well. They charged me with armed robbery home invasion. I sat in jail for 30 days—innocent and afraid.

After I was released from jail on bond, I was placed under house arrest for six months—from July, when I got out of jail, to January, when my court date was scheduled. I fell into a deep depression and was prescribed Xanax under my parents' care. While I was under house arrest, I attended church with my mom for only one reason: to get out of the house. Before long, I found that I liked the message, but I still wasn't convinced that God existed.

One Sunday after the service had finished, my mom grabbed my hand and pulled me towards the prayer team. A few members of the team began to pray over me. Even though I was really loopy and I don't remember exactly what they said that night, I know I apologized to God for my sins.

I vividly remember waking up the next morning and feeling God's presence. I thought to myself, "I don't need my Xanax or my depression medication anymore. I'm free!" I felt so empowered that I threw all my pills in the garbage. I no longer felt any chains holding me back. That morning I saw my old self through God's eyes, and I instantly knew that I was no longer the same person. The most amazing thing was that after four years of medicating myself with narcotics, marijuana, and anti-depressants, I didn't have a single symptom of withdrawal.

At my court date in January, I pled to a lesser charge and received only probation. I was happy to find out that the church I attended with my mom was a place where I could do my community service for my probation. As I served, I began to grow deeper in my faith.

Then I heard about the World Race. It's an eleven-month, eleven-country mission trip spanning four continents. I immediately knew that God wanted me to go; however, I wasn't sure if I could because the race would begin three weeks before my probation was scheduled to end. And beyond that, I wasn't sure if the World Race would accept me because of my criminal record. I put in my application anyway, prayed like crazy, and trusted God to work it all out.

After what seemed like forever to me, I received the phone call I had been waiting for—I was accepted! I also found out that because I had been completing my community service, attending my drug classes, and staying clean, I could petition for early termination of my probation. I didn't have money for an attorney, so I went in front of the judge by myself.

"I'm a changed woman," I told the judge, "and I'm going to change the world."

Amazingly, the judge honored my request, and I was released from probation early. I praised God for all the doors He had opened for me.

In January, I left for Honduras and began an amazing year. While on the mission field, our team evangelized, performed community outreach, built churches, did street ministry, and provided medical relief. On a personal level, getting to see couples serving together revealed to me a higher standard for relationships. I realized that my previous relationships had everything but number one—God. At that point I decided to seek only godly relationships. If He wasn't number one, the relationship wasn't going to work.

I felt fulfilled when the mission trip ended, but I felt myself missing the people I had served. After I returned home, I stayed in touch with the locals. They kept asking if I could send more teams. I started thinking to myself that it was not just about sending teams, but about teaching the local people to become self-sufficient. As the saying goes "If you give a man a fish, you feed him for a day, but if you teach him how to fish, you feed him for a lifetime." I wanted these people to learn how to fish.

After pondering and praying over how I could help, I decided to start a nonprofit called Four Letter Word that focuses on the elimination of global poverty. The mission of Four Letter Word is to provide resources and education as well as to empower both individuals and communities to build healthy, self-sustainable habitats. We are now in the process of setting up chicken farms to help orphanages raise chickens for both a source of income and a source of food.

Sometimes in life we question why we go through storms. I know for me that all the challenges in my life have made me who I am today. If I hadn't hit rock-bottom, I may never have let my mom drag me to church. I wouldn't have gone to the prayer team, and I wouldn't have experienced the presence of God in my life that ultimately broke the chains of addiction. I had no clue how God was going to use me or that He even *could* use me. The transformation that He brought about in my life has allowed me to help bring transformation in the lives of others.

For we are God's handiwork, created in Christ Jesus to do good works, which God prepared in advance for us to do. Ephesians 2:10

Connect With The Contributing Author

Rayna is the president of Four Letter Word. She is passionate about eliminating hunger, poverty, and disease.
Website: www.fourletterword.org
E-mail: raynajoy@fourletterword.org
facebook.com/4lword
twitter.com/4lword
instagram.com/4lword

Transformed Reflection Questions

1. According to *Merriam-Webster,* one of the definitions of transformation is "to change in character or condition." We've seen many examples of transformation in this section. Think back over your life. What transformations can you recognize?

   _____

   _____

   _____

   _____

2. A transformer provides energy to a home. If the transformer goes out, the end result is no energy—no electricity—no power. We need that transformer to bring us power to perform many of our daily activities. Can you think of ways that God is or could be your transformer?

   _____

   _____

   _____

   _____

3. In this section you've read accounts of people who were transformed and then went on to impact their communities. How are YOU impacting those around you?

   _____

Question 3 continued

_____

_____

_____

4. In *The Biggest Loser...Ever,* Danny wrote a list of things entitled "What to do to achieve my dreams?" If you wrote a similar list, what would it look like?

_____

_____

_____

_____

Challenge

Complete this sentence: I would like to ask God to transform my _____. If you would like to share your answer, please post to our Facebook page (www.facebook.com/Godincidence) or Twitter account (@God_Incidence) with the hashtag #CoincidenceChallenge.

BLESSED

Introduction to Blessed

In the previous sections, you have encountered some amazing stories of how God has changed lives by rescuing people, revealing Himself, and then transforming hearts. In this section you will discover stories of ordinary people—secretaries, grandmothers, work-at-home-moms, college students, and businessmen—who all believe that God is blessing their lives.

The Bible tells us the story of a widow in 2 Kings 4. Her husband had passed away, and his creditors were coming to collect her two sons as slaves to pay off the debts. She sought out the prophet of God, Elisha, to ask him what she should do. He asked her what she had in her house to sell, and she told him that she had only a small jar of oil.

³ Elisha said, "Go around and ask all your neighbors for empty jars. Don't ask for just a few. ⁴ Then go inside and shut the door behind you and your sons. Pour oil into all the jars, and as each is filled, put it to one side."

⁵ She left him and shut the door behind her and her sons. They brought the jars to her and she kept pouring. ⁶ When all the jars were full, she said to her son, "Bring me another one." But he replied, "There is not a jar left." Then the oil stopped flowing.

⁷ She went and told the man of God, and he said, "Go, sell the oil and pay your debts. You and your sons can live on what is left."

Much like the widow, you might feel like you don't have anything to give. Your debts may be mounting, your health may be failing, or you may find yourself in the throes of grief. When troublesome times come, it's easy to question God and fail to see His care and provision. Even though the widow was between a rock and a hard place, she still had enough faith to seek out Elisha and ask what to do. As a result of her faith and belief in God, she was abundantly blessed with more than enough money to save her sons. She didn't doubt that God would provide a solution.

It's easy to recognize the big blessing in the widow's story and in stories like *The Biggest Loser...Ever* and *Victim to Victor*. However, blessings can come in all shapes and sizes.

Let's face it. Parents can't take their children to an amusement park every single day as a demonstration of their love, but they can shower their children with hugs, kisses, and words of appreciation on a regular basis. Those tiny acts of love can make a huge difference in a child's life. God reveals His love to us in the same way—through the daily, seemingly mundane things of life. How often do you recognize and acknowledge those blessings?

The stories in this section reveal how God orchestrates even the tiniest details of our lives in order to grant us blessings. You will read how a small child was blessed by God for a selfless act of charity, how an unexpected car repair demonstrated God's providence, and how God can resurrect hope after a devastating loss.

After reading these stories, we hope that you will begin to recognize the small ways in which God shows His unceasing love toward you. Remember that His love is faithful and unconditional and that He cares about you no matter what has happened in your past.

Easter Blessings

Lisa Crumbley

Every Easter, my family had a tradition of dyeing Easter eggs at my parents' house. My dad always made the craziest, ugliest egg, and the kids looked forward to seeing the egg that Poppie made because it was known as the "fifty cent money egg." He would make three types of eggs: one with ten cents, one with twenty-five cents, and the ugliest egg was the fifty cent egg. He would write on the egg with the wax crayon that comes in the dye kit—the kind with the writing that can't be seen until the egg is actually dipped in the color. Poppie would dip his fingers into the dye and then put the dye on the egg. Somehow the eggs always turned out an ugly shade of grey, but Poppie said it was to camouflage them so they wouldn't be easy to find.

One particular Easter, my son JJ, who was dressed in a light sky blue jacket with matching bow tie, was about five years old—old enough to be excited about the money eggs. As the kids started hunting, Poppie jingled the money in his pocket, making the hunt more exciting for the kids because they could actually hear the reward waiting. JJ was thrilled when he found some of the money eggs! He went running over to Poppie to collect his sixty cents in change. It was almost like Christmas morning to JJ. He collected his two quarters and one dime and carefully put them into his pocket for safe-keeping.

After the early morning egg hunt at my parents' house, we headed off to meet my husband's family for church. When it came time for the collection, the adults in our row put their donations in the plate and started to pass the plate around JJ.

"Wait, wait!" JJ exclaimed. "I have something to put in this time for the poor people!"

I watched as his little five-year-old hands reached into his pants pocket and purposefully placed each coin that Poppie had given him into the collection plate. Two quarters and one shiny dime. He wasn't boastful or proud—just matter-of-fact—as a wide smile spread across his face.

After church we drove to Grandma and Grandpa's house for lunch and another Easter egg hunt with my husband's family. To our surprise, Grandpa had placed money in some of the plastic eggs. Even though seven children hunted for those eggs, JJ found every one that had money inside. His total? $1.80—exactly three times what he had just placed in the church collection plate. I sincerely believe that God rewarded this cheerful giver!

———— ∾ ·· ∾ ————

⁶ Remember this: Whoever sows sparingly will also reap sparingly,
and whoever sows generously will also reap generously.
⁷ Each of you should give what you have decided in your heart to give,
not reluctantly or under compulsion, for God loves a cheerful giver.
2 Corinthians 9:6–7

Connect With The Contributing Author
Lisa is an author, speaker, and former radio host.
Website: www.coincidencethebook.com
E-mail: lisa@coincidencethebook.com

I've Got Your Back

Blaine Albright

Driving down the road and noticing the dreaded "Check Engine" light never results in a good feeling. However, back in the summer of 2012, I would have appreciated the "Check Engine" light turning on in my vehicle. Instead of giving any warning, my (by all other accounts) perfectly reliable, relatively new car started shutting down while I was driving it—once on the interstate and another time in the middle of an intersection with two of my young children in the car. I drove my car to the mechanic, and after much testing, he finally figured out what the problem was.

I had hoped that the issue might be covered under the vehicle's warranty, but it wasn't. I even wrote a letter to the car manufacturer asking for help with this dangerous issue. (A quick Internet search had informed me that I wasn't the first to experience this issue.) Unfortunately, the manufacturer didn't respond, so I eventually paid for the part and went on my way.

Two years later, I was cleaning and organizing my garage when I happened upon the receipt for those repairs. I was curious to know if the issue had persisted and been addressed by the car manufacturer, so I did another quick Internet search. I learned that the faulty part had, in fact, been recalled just a few months before, but a lot of fine print detailed who qualified for a repair or refund. I called the phone number listed and was directed to a website that gave instructions for requesting a reimbursement if the part had been replaced and paid for out-of-pocket. A full refund seemed a little too good to be true, so after submitting the forms, I moved on and didn't really think about whether anything would come of it.

A few weeks later, I knew one of my tires needed to be replaced, so I went to the mechanic again. What I didn't know was that my car needed more than one tire—plus another costly repair! My total amounted to $419. This unexpected expense felt a little bit like a punch in the stomach because it came on the heels of one of my boys needing braces and another needing stitches. As I was tempted to freak out about the impending pile of bills, I was reminded by both the Holy Spirit and my faithful wife, Alexis, that God wasn't surprised by any of this. I felt Him saying, "I've got your back. Trust Me."

When I returned home, my wife showed me a check that arrived in the mail that day. It was the refund from the car manufacturer for the recalled part and repair. When I looked at the check, I could barely speak. It was for $419 exactly!

While God could have used any way He wanted to provide for our family, I'm thankful that He chose to show His providence in a way that strengthened my faith and affirmed His care for me. He knew exactly what we would need and exactly when we would need it!

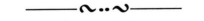

And my God will supply every need of yours
according to his riches in glory in Christ Jesus. Philippians 4:19 (ESV)

A Small Package

Mary Beth Cinfici

Not too long ago, I was diagnosed with MDS, a form of blood cancer. Through this scary time in my life, I turned to my friend Becky, whose husband had gone through cancer treatment, and she gave me much-needed support and encouragement.

Before I started my treatments, my doctors inserted a port under my skin near my left collarbone so I could receive blood transfusions and chemotherapy without having my arm stuck with needles. Because of the port's location, the safety belt in my car rubbed against it. My job was a forty-five-minute drive from my home, and the rubbing of the belt against the port made my commute very uncomfortable.

One day, as I was driving home from work, I started thinking and praying about what I could do to stop the safety belt from making the skin around my port so sore. I hadn't told anyone, not even Becky, about the discomfort I was feeling.

When I arrived home and picked up my mail, I found a small package from Becky. Inside was a little pillow with a note attached that said she thought it would help me while I was driving because she remembered how difficult it was for her husband to drive when he had his port. All

I had to do was place the pillow under my safety belt and over my port.

That little pillow was the perfect gift at just the right time. What an amazing illustration of how God answers our prayers. He knows exactly what we need and sends his blessings in packages of all sizes.

Answer me when I call, O God of my righteousness!
You have given me relief when I was in distress.
Be gracious to me and hear my prayer! Psalm 4:1 (ESV)

———⌁⸱⸱⌁———
An Unexpected Tip

Sandra Richardson

———⌁⸱⸱⌁———

I'm a college student, and I don't want to graduate with a lot of debt to repay. To keep my head above water, I work as a waitress.

My boyfriend's parents told me about Dave Ramsey's Financial Peace University, which is a curriculum that teaches people how to budget, dump debt, and win with money. They were teaching the course in a small group in their home. My boyfriend's parents had recently gone through the course and said that it had changed their lives, and they invited me to attend.

The only problem was that the course cost $110. That might not seem like a lot of money to you, but to a broke college student it may as well have been $1,000. When I shared my concern with my boyfriend's mom, she told me about scholarships that were available through the church that would cover half the cost. I would only have to pay $55, and my boyfriend's parents were willing to pitch in to bring my cost down to $40.

I went to work on a Saturday night hoping to bring home $100 in tips. I really wanted to be able to cover the $55 cost by myself and still have enough money left over to eat. The restaurant I work at is on the water, and it was a beautiful evening, so I was very hopeful because on a good night I could make up to $200.

The next day I went over to my boyfriend's parents' house to sign up for the class. When his mom took out her wallet to pay the $15 she promised, I said—

"I've got this! I received a tip at work last night that paid for my class!"

It was a large party, and they had left me a tip of exactly $55. Not only that, but I left work that night with $155 in my pocket—the original $100 I had hoped for plus the additional $55 to cover the class.

And we will receive from him whatever we ask because
we obey him and do the things that please him. 1 John 3:22 (NLT)

—— ᜈ ·· ᜈ ——

One in a Million

Kara Starcher

—— ᜈ ·· ᜈ ——

I reached out for the bathroom counter as a sudden excruciating pain ripped through my abdomen. "This must be the kidney stone passing," I thought to myself as I tried to straighten up.

Earlier that day, my midwife had told me the source of the occasional twinge of pain I was feeling during the first few weeks of my pregnancy was likely a kidney stone. The ultrasound showed a normal pregnancy, so I just had to wait for the kidney stone to pass. The midwife said it would be painful when it passed, and this was definitely, without a doubt, painful.

Then the nausea and vomiting hit. "Oh great, 'morning' sickness at night. Let's add to the fun."

After a few minutes, I felt a bit better and crawled into bed for the night. I thought about calling Ron, who was working away from home on the oil & gas pipeline. I wanted to tell him about the kidney stone, but I knew that at 11 p.m. he was already asleep in his hotel room. I would have to tell him in the morning. Little did I know that only by God's grace would I survive to see the morning.

Around 4:30 a.m. I awoke in overwhelming pain. Feeling nauseous, I made my way to the bathroom. When I finished emptying the contents of my stomach, I stood up and looked at myself in the mirror. I was horrified to realize I was an unnatural gray color. Something wasn't right, and I knew I needed help.

"Dear God, don't let me die here alone. Keep my baby safe. Help some of this pain go away! Please!"

I slowly made my way back to the bed where the phone was resting on the nightstand. I thought about calling Ron's mom who lived a few miles away, but I knew that if I called her before 5:00 a.m. she would instantly panic thinking something serious had happened to Ron. I considered driving myself to the ER, but the closest hospital was twenty-five miles away and the pain was getting more intense. So, I dialed Ron's number. I explained what was going on and asked him to call his mom to come take me to the ER.

A few minutes later, I propped myself against the inside of the back door watching for car headlights to come up the gravel road. I could feel my body getting weaker.

After Ron's mom arrived, we headed for the hospital. We made quite a few stops along the side of the road so I could dry heave, and after what seemed like forever, we pulled into the hospital parking lot. I tried to stand up straight after I exited the car, but the severe pain forced me to walk bent over with my arm putting pressure on my abdomen. While Ron's mom parked the car, I slowly walked from the drop-off area to the emergency room entrance. As I reached out my hand to push the buzzer on the ER door, it opened. "Is your back bothering you, honey?" a nurse asked. Then she looked me in the eye. "No, it's not your back, is it? You don't look right. Come back here to a bed."

The next hour was a flurry of activity. Because the rural hospital didn't have a labor and delivery ward, and the closest OBGYN was over fifty miles away, the ER called one of the local physicians who happened to be a former OBGYN. When Dr. Masters arrived, he briefly introduced himself and told me that the ER doctor had called the sonographer in as well. As soon as she arrived, I would have another ultrasound to see if they could figure out what was going on. Dr. Masters then left to make some phone calls and have copies of my records faxed to him at the hospital.

By now, the pain was searing through my shoulders, rendering my arms almost useless. I could barely move on the hospital bed, and it was impossible to get comfortable.

After a bit, a nurse returned with an aide who was pushing a wheelchair to take me to the ultrasound room. I very slowly maneuvered myself to a semi-standing position and then turned to sit in the wheelchair. As I sat down, I felt myself pitch forward and the room went black. I woke to find myself laying on the hospital bed. My room was full of hospital personnel.

Since sitting in the wheelchair was obviously out of the question, an aide pushed my hospital bed to the ultrasound room. Dr. Masters entered the room after us and explained that the sonographer would check as many of my organs as possible to see if they could find the source of my pain. She would start with a vaginal ultrasound to check the baby.

I have two distinct memories from the ultrasound room. The first is of digging my nails into Dr. Masters's arm, likely to the point of drawing blood, as I screamed in pain. The other is the look of confusion on the sonographer's face when she looked at the monitor. Nothing was distinguishable. My abdomen looked like a snowy television screen—it was completely filled with fluid.

Dr. Masters explained that I was experiencing a ruptured ectopic, or tubal, pregnancy. I would need emergency surgery to stop the internal bleeding. The surgeon would insert a scope through my belly button and repair the damage.

When I arrived back in my ER room, an EMT was sitting in a chair in the corner. He didn't say a word—he just sat there.

Around 8:30 a.m., a nurse came in and told me that the ER doctor had called the surgeon who was in his office across the parking lot. As soon as the surgeon arrived, I would be sent to the operating room.

Time passed. I asked where the surgeon was. They said he was coming.

The clock continued to tick. Around 10:15, I glanced at the blood pressure monitor. One of the numbers read 32. I looked at the EMT who was sitting stoically in the corner. In a not-so-nice tone I said, "How about you get up off of your chair and do something? Go walk across the parking lot and get that surgeon since he obviously doesn't understand that I'm dying. It doesn't take two hours to walk across a parking lot. Do you want me to die while you sit in that chair?"

Over twelve hours after my tube ruptured and five hours after entering the ER, the surgeon finally showed up. Since I had bled internally for twelve hours, the simple laparoscopic surgery wasn't possible, and I ended up undergoing a laparotomy complete with a five-inch vertical incision.

Later that evening, the surgeon came to my hospital room to see how

I was doing. He apologized to me and said he didn't realize that what the ER personnel kept calling "emergency surgery" was really, in fact, an emergency. I said a silent prayer thanking God that even with the surgeon's lack of urgency He chose to spare my life.

Dr. Masters came to visit as well. He explained the details of the surgery and that I would likely need another blood transfusion the next day because I had lost over half of my blood volume. He was amazed that I had been able to fall asleep the night before after the rupture occurred. (The rupture was actually the searing pain that I had assumed was the kidney stone.) He was even more amazed that I woke up hours later. He told me to rest and he would be back the next day to visit.

Reality set in as I lay in my dark room by myself. Our baby was gone. I cried myself to sleep.

Early the next morning, Dr. Masters came back to see me, as he would every day I was in the hospital. He sat by my bedside and talked with me about how to deal with the grief and about what had happened in the previous weeks leading up to the rupture. My biggest point of confusion was the seemingly normal ultrasound from a few days before.

"Sometimes when a baby is embedded in a tube, a pseudo sac forms in the uterus. On an ultrasound, the sac and its contents appear to be similar to the early stages of a fetus' development."

"Could it have been twins?" I asked.

"It would be very, very rare, but it can happen. However, I doubt it. Why do you ask?"

I explained that my paternal grandfather was a twin which meant I was genetically in line to have twins. I had done quite a bit of ancestral research and knew that other twins were in my family tree as well. I also added the fact that Ron's extended family had five sets of twins alive at the time. I didn't tell Dr. Masters but I knew in my heart of hearts that I now had twin angel babies in heaven.

"I guess with your grandfather being a twin, it is a miniscule possibility that it may have been twins."

We talked for a bit more about twins and genetics, and then Dr. Masters shifted gears.

"Assuming you want to try to conceive again, you need to realize that your chances are very slim. I know you believe in God, and with God nothing is impossible, but because of the little bit of history that I know and the extensive damage done to your body, you have about a *one in a million* chance of getting pregnant naturally. It's very likely that you will experience infertility issues and need assistance getting pregnant." Dr. Masters continued to outline the damage done to my body and what that meant for my future.

Tears silently fell down my cheeks. Not only were my babies gone, but now it looked like any hope of future children was questionable too.

I spent four days in the hospital and about six weeks recovering at home from the surgery as well as the significant blood loss. The grief of losing our babies plus knowing that I may not have other children was overwhelming at times. During those first few weeks, I cried and questioned God a lot. I was thankful that He had spared my life but couldn't understand why He had allowed the problem to be missed on the first ultrasound. If it was missed once, who's to say it wouldn't be missed again?

Initially, I was terrified of becoming pregnant again. Having stared death in the face once, I had no immediate desire to repeat the experience. Dr. Masters recommended waiting a minimum of three months, but ideally, for the best possible outcome with a pregnancy, I should wait six months before attempting to get pregnant again.

In early June, I went for my seven-month post-surgery follow up visit with Dr. Masters. He gave me a big hug and told me how thankful he was to see me looking so healthy. By this time I had come to a certain amount of peace over losing our babies. I still ached with grief, especially since my original due date was a few weeks away, but I was okay. Dr. Masters and I discussed again the road that may be ahead of me if I should decide to try for another pregnancy. Since the cause of my ectopic pregnancy was never determined, the danger existed that I could have another one. So, Dr. Masters submitted a standing order to the laboratory for pregnancy blood work. I was to go in immediately if I had a positive pregnancy test. He also reminded me not to get my hopes up because my chances were one in a million.

About two weeks later I was in the laboratory getting blood work done. Afterwards, I went upstairs to Dr. Masters's office and left a note for him.

> *"Dear Dr. Masters,*
> *I just wanted you to know that I had a positive pregnancy test and had my blood work done today. With God nothing is impossible!"*

The next day, my phone rang. "Hi Kara, it's Dr. Masters. I checked your labs, and they came back as positive for pregnancy! Congratulations!"

"Doc, do you know what day today is? June 28. My original due date. You couldn't have given me better news."

"Well, amen!" I could hear the pleasure in Dr. Master's voice. "Like your note said, nothing is impossible. God just gave you a big blessing. But first let's make sure everything is okay this time. I scheduled you for an ultrasound tomorrow morning."

Early the next morning, on my thirty-fourth birthday, I walked into the ultrasound room. The sonographer was very thorough and explained exactly what I was seeing on the screen. At four weeks and six days gestation, it was a bit too early to hear a heartbeat, but there was a tiny hint of a flutter on the screen. Then came the moment I'll never forget.

"Wait a minute...," the sonographer said.

"Oh no!" I thought. My heart plummeted and a feeling of dread washed over me. "This is it. This is where she tells me that something is wrong. Why, God? Why does this have to happen?"

I felt the tears start to well up behind my eyes. I couldn't endure another loss so soon. I thought I was ready, but I wasn't.

"See this right here?" She pointed to a faint gray blob on the screen. "I think it might be a twin."

"Twin?" My voice squeaked a little.

"I can't be 100% sure because it's very early, but I've been doing these ultrasounds for years and this definitely looks like a twin."

I stared at the screen. I had a hard time distinguishing what she was pointing at. It certainly didn't look like another baby.

She said she was marking it for the radiologist to look at as she typed, "Possible twin?"

A few minutes later while I was in the changing room, the sonographer checked my lab work which indicated that my HcG levels were higher than normal—a sign of a stable twin pregnancy. However, we had to wait another six weeks for the next ultrasound to confirm that I was carrying twins and hadn't experienced Vanishing Twin Syndrome, where one twin simply disappears without any medical explanation or miscarriage symptoms.

Just over seven months later, at thirty-seven weeks, we welcomed two beautiful, healthy baby girls into our family. Two years later, we would welcome another little girl.

God allowed the ruptured ectopic pregnancy and my brush with death to happen, and I don't doubt that He orchestrated the details. He gave me a compassionate Christian doctor, who just *happened* to have practiced as an OBGYN, to guide me through those initial dark days of grief and pain. Only God could have arranged it so that I would receive confirmation of a new pregnancy on my original due date, despite all the odds that were stacked against me. And then to see two babies instead of one, on my birthday nonetheless, was beyond my wildest expectations.

Jesus looked at them and said,
"With man this is impossible, but not with God;
all things are possible with God." Mark 10:27

Blessed Reflection Questions

1. Have you ever felt compelled to bless someone in an unexpected way? Did you follow your instinct or did you ignore it? How did it make you feel?

   _____

   _____

   _____

   _____

2. In the introduction we discussed how God cares for even the tiniest details. Can you attribute a tiny detail of your life to a God-incidence that you may not have viewed that way before?

   _____

   _____

   _____

   _____

3. Galatians 6:7 says, "Do not be deceived: God cannot be mocked. A man reaps what he sows." In other words, what goes around comes around. In what ways have you reaped what you've sown?

   _____

   _____

   _____

4. In the stories *I've Got Your Back* and *An Unexpected Tip*, the contributing authors talk about financial blessings that they believed were from God. What types of blessings have you received that you believe came from God?

_____

_____

_____

_____

Challenge

Think back over the last week and write down how you've seen God bless you in big and small ways. We would love for you to share your thoughts on our Facebook page (www.facebook.com/Godincidence) or Twitter account (@God_Incidence) using the hashtag #CoincidenceChallenge.

—— ∽ .. ∽ ——
Where Do I Go from Here?
—— ∽ .. ∽ ——

In the beginning of the book, we posed a question to you. We asked:

Does God exist?

After reading our contributing authors' true stories, has your answer changed? If you were a seeker, hopefully their stories provided some evidence to you that God exists.

As evidenced by many of the stories you read, following God's plan for your life isn't always easy. But, one thing that all of our contributing authors would tell you is that God's love never fails. Even when negative words are flooding your mind, God and His love are still there available for you to reach out and take.

We live in dark and difficult times. We believe the lies that the devil whispers in our ears. We hear words like *unworthy, unqualified, forgotten, abandoned, ashamed,* and *unforgiven.* We try to forge ahead on our own, doing things our way. We forget that God speaks the truth through His word. He calls us *worthy, qualified, remembered, adopted, unashamed,* and *forgiven.* He also tells us in 1 Peter 5:8 to "Stay alert!

Watch out for your great enemy, the devil. He prowls around like a roaring lion, looking for someone to devour." (NLT)

Are you going to allow the devil and society to devour you? Are you going to believe those negative words? Or are you going to continue studying and researching God's ways of living and allow Him to transform you?

Are you tired of trying to do things all on your own? Are you ready to stop trusting your own feelings and to start trusting the truth from God and His word?

If God is missing from your life, you can invite Him in and allow Him to start transforming your life. Peter tells us in Acts 2:38–41 that we need to "'Repent and be baptized, every one of you, in the name of Jesus Christ for the forgiveness of your sins. And you will receive the gift of the Holy Spirit. The promise is for you and your children and for all who are far off—for all whom the Lord our God will call.' With many other words he [Peter] warned them; and he pleaded with them, 'Save yourselves from this corrupt generation.'"

Maybe you are feeling alone in your faith journey and can't see your way through the confusion of the devil's lies. Matthew 18:20 states, "For where two or three gather in my name, there am I with them." Some of our authors told how they, sometimes reluctantly, set foot inside of a church. To their surprise, they felt God's presence once they stepped inside the doors. Through regular attendance, they came to understand God and His plan for their lives.

If you desire more information about God or the Bible, we have compiled a list of websites, books, and mobile apps that may provide the answers you are looking for. You can find the list in *Resources*.

Share Your Story

Has something happened in your life that you thought no one else would ever believe?

Throughout the course of researching this book, we had people tell us their seemingly unbelievable stories, but they asked us not to print them because they didn't want their friends and family to think they were crazy. We believe that God works in all kinds of ways, just like you've read in the stories of this book.

Every one of us has a story to tell, and we believe that by sharing your story your words can bring hope and healing to others. Another benefit that we've discovered in our journey to write this book is that sharing your story can also bring healing to you, the storyteller, as we have seen happen in *Healing from My Secret Sin*.

Don't let fear stop you from sharing what God has done for you. He calls us to be His witnesses about the wonderful way that He weaves everything in our lives all together for His good.

Come and listen, all you who have respect for God.
Let me tell you what he has done for me. Psalm 66:16 (NIrV)

If you would like to share your story for possible future publication, please visit our website **CoincidenceTheBook.com** and click on the "Submit" tab.

Resources

If you desire to learn more about God or the Bible, consider the following resources.

Websites

AnswersInGenesis.org – An apologetics ministry to help Christians defend their faith and proclaim the gospel of Jesus Christ effectively

BibleHub.com – Online Bible Study Suite: Topical, Greek and Hebrew study tools, plus concordances, commentaries, sermons and devotionals

BibleGateway.com – Devotionals, Bible reading plans, and mobile apps

Biblia.com – An online Bible study tool with dozens of Bibles for your Bible study needs

Proverbs31.org – Bringing God's peace, perspective, and purpose to today's busy woman

RightNowMedia.org – Described by Matt Chandler, Lead Pastor of

The Village Church, as "The Netflix of Christian Bible Study"

SheReadsTruth.com – Women in the Word of God every day

HeReadsTruth.com – Men in the Word of God every day

Mobile Apps

Many of the websites listed above also offer mobile apps.

YouVersion Bible: YouVersion.com/apps – Take the Bible with you wherever you go

First 5: First5.org – Transform your time with God

Daughters of the King: Dot-k.com – Daily devotional

Books

The Case For Christ by Lee Stroebel

Purpose Driven Life by Rick Warren

Disclaimer: We have no affiliation or association with these resources and may or may not agree with the views expressed within. We are simply recommending them to you for your personal study.

———∿..∿———

"Coincidence is God's way of remaining anonymous."

- Author Unknown

———∿..∿———